CREATIVE CARD PLAY

The Cure For Unimaginative Bridge!

By James S. Kauder

Foreword by

Mike Lawrence,

World Bridge Champion

Lawrence & Leong Publishing

Printed in the United States of America

Lawrence & Leong Publishing
10430 Greenview Drive
Oakland, California 94605

Library of Congress Catalog Card Number: 89-80898

ISBN 1-877908-00-2

THE EXPERT'S SECTION

FOREWORD

ALMOST 25 YEARS AGO I MET JIMMY KAUDER at a regional in Los Angeles. Initially we were a bit wary of each other because our moments together were always as adversaries each trying to beat the other. Fortunately this state of affairs changed and we got to know each other as friends instead of opponents.

It turns out that we have more in common than anyone could imagine. As an eighteen year old freshman in college, I made a chemical compound (sorry, no recipes) which turned out to be more volatile than I had anticipated. It exploded leaving me to this day with a stain on my right hand. Thirty years later people tease me about having a leaky pen. Amazingly, Jimmy did the same thing with the identical substance when he was eighteen. Further comparisons showed a number of similar inclinations. We like the same food, we have the same interests, we both like solving the mysteries of bridge, and we have the same wry sense of humor.

When he told me years ago that he was writing a bridge book, I asked to see the manuscript in progress. He could hardly wait to show it to me. I loved it.

Eventually, Jim did publish his book and I am pleased to say I have an autographed original. Sadly, Jim's book somehow found it's way out of print. That has been corrected. It's back.

Originally, Jim's book was published under the title "The Bridge Philosopher". That title described the spirit behind the book, but it didn't reveal the true contents. Creative Card Play is a compilation of good thought provoking bridge hands which should be solved at the table. I've read a number of bridge books, and I judge their merit on presentation and on what I can learn from them. Creative Card Play has a style which will appeal to many, which will raise a few eyebrows, but which will get everyone's attention. I was often reminded of a lesson I wished I had learned earlier which is to keep an open mind. The inevitable doesn't have to happen!

I enjoyed reading this book. The hands ranged from interesting to perplexing to intriguing. There was always an impetus to read the next sentence. I especially appreciated that this book had useful themes which I haven't seen elsewhere. For example: In the hand titled "The Tired Man" you are in three notrump and you need three tricks from AQ7 opposite J954. To this day I have been waiting for it. I'm ready. I'm not going to tell you how to do it. Look it up. You'll be surprised.

MIKE LAWRENCE
July, 1989

PREFACE

I HAVE BEEN PLAYING BRIDGE for more than thirty years. I have played bridge in all sorts of places, among them being Los Angeles, San Francisco, Phoenix, Chicago, and New York City. I have played in dives, private homes, and in the most elegant of card clubs, for fun and profit.

Whenever I played, I seem to run into the same type of characters: Tired Men who pushed themselves to the point of exhaustion playing bridge for long hours, Unlucky Players who continuously bemoaned their poor luck, and Gamblers who lost their rent money and more playing bridge for stakes they could not afford.

This book was intended to be instructive as to play and defense and to amuse the reader with a few anecdotes. It was also intended to introduce the many characters who inhabit the bridge world. Just take a look around you the next time you play. You'll have no trouble identifying the Gossips, the pugnacious Married Couples, the Friendly Men, and the Needlers. Many bridge players fit into these categories, yet each is unique. Each contributes his own particular hue to the spectrum of humanity that makes up the world of bridge.

JAMES S. KAUDER
July, 1989

A SIMPLE HAND

THIS IS A SIMPLE HAND. Yet, not one player I've shown it to has played the hand correctly, dear reader. See how you do with it.

Playing rubber bridge, I hold as South:

♠ AKQ   ♡ AK6   ◇ AQ874   ♣ K2

I open the bidding with Three No Trump. All Pass, so the bidding has been:

NORTH	EAST	SOUTH	WEST
—	—	3NT	Pass
Pass	Pass		

West leads the five of hearts and North puts down this dummy:

NORTH
♠ 654
♡ 972
◇ J1093
♣ 654

SOUTH
♠ AKQ
♡ AK6
◇ AQ874
♣ K2

Dummy plays low on the first heart, East the queen and I win the king. I have nine top tricks after forcing out the king of diamonds. The only way I can be set is if East wins the king of diamonds and shifts to a club.

With no entry to dummy, the normal way to play the diamonds is to play the ace and another diamond to dummy's jack. This gains a trick whenever the king is a singleton. But I see a snag in playing the diamonds this way. West might hold a singleton diamond and discard a heart on the second diamond, making it easier for East to find the killing club shift. Therefore, I lead a low diamond to dummy's jack at trick two.

The complete hand:

```
                    NORTH
                    ♠ 654
                    ♡ 972
                    ◇ J1093
                    ♣ 654
   WEST                              EAST
   ♠ J32                            ♠ 10987
   ♡ J10853                         ♡ Q4
   ◇ 2                              ◇ K65
   ♣ AQJ3                           ♣ 10987
                    SOUTH
                    ♠ AKQ
                    ♡ AK6
                    ◇ AQ874
                    ♣ K2
```

If declarer plays ace and another diamond, East can hold up the king and win the third round. West meanwhile should pitch a low heart and a low spade, to direct a club switch.

However, if declarer begins with a low diamond to dummy's jack, East would have to be a genius to find the club switch.

Hand 2

NO OPTION

I NEVER LIKE TO SEE A HAND PASSED OUT when the opponents have a part score. To my mind that gives the opponents two chances to make game instead of one.

This hand is from a four deal rubber bridge game. On the fourth deal with both sides vulnerable I pick up:

♠ J1092   ♡ A82   ◇ 42   ♣ AJ92

The opponents have a part score of 90. Partner passes and East passes and it's my bid.

This is a situation I never like. I hate to open so light in third seat, but if I pass, then I give West the option of opening or passing the bidding out. And he'll open the bidding only when he holds a reasonable hand. When the hand belongs to us at Two Hearts or Two Spades then West will be glad to pass the hand out.

I'm not going to give West that option. If he's going to complete the part score, he is going to have to do it on this hand. Besides, with four deuces I probably hold the best poker hand at the table.

I open One Club. West passes and partner responds One Diamond. No choice. I have to rebid One Spade. Now partner raises me to Four Spades. What has he done! I brace myself for a Double. Fortunately, it never comes.

The auction has been:

NORTH	EAST	SOUTH	WEST
Pass	Pass	1♣	Pass
1♢	Pass	1♠	Pass
4♠	Pass	Pass	Pass

West leads the queen of diamonds. Partner proudly displays:

NORTH
♠ AK43
♡ K4
♢ K85
♣ 8543

SOUTH
♠ J1092
♡ A82
♢ 42
♣ AJ92

Why partner didn't open that hand is beyond me. And especially with the opponents having 90 below. He probably didn't want to open "for a part score." Yes, I've heard that story before. It would have served him right if I had passed him in One Diamond.

I cover the queen of diamonds with dummy's king. East wins the ace and return the three of diamonds to West's ten. West tries to cash the jack of diamonds, but I ruff.

I lead the jack of spades. West gives this card his customary pause, which likely shows that he doesn't hold the queen. If he held the queen he'd duck smoothly, so I go with dummy's ace and East drops the eight.

I've played against my right hand opponent numerous times and I have yet to see him falsecard. The missing spot cards in the trump suit are the 8-7-6-5, and of course they should be played at random. But East never falsecards, hence his play of the eight can be only be from the queen-eight doubleton or the singleton eight. I'll have to play him for the queen-eight doubleton, for if he holds the singleton eight then West will have a natural trump trick.

I cash dummy's king of spades and East drops the queen. Both opponents appear unhappy at this. I lead a club to the nine and West wins the king. He exits with a heart which I win in hand. I pull the last trump with my jack and return to dummy with the king of hearts.

When I lead a club from the dummy East plays the seven. He's done it again! I already know that he holds the ten of clubs. Now, if he holds the queen as well, then I must lose a club trick even if I successfully finesse the jack. My only chance to make Four Spades is to play the ace of clubs. I am fortunate enough to drop the queen, for the complete hand is:

NORTH
♠ AK43
♡ K4
◇ K85
♣ 8543

WEST
♠ 765
♡ J653
◇ QJ106
♣ KQ

EAST
♠ Q8
♡ Q1097
◇ A753
♣ 1076

SOUTH
♠ J1092
♡ A82
◇ 42
♣ AJ92

This time the opponents were really suffering. Partner, on the other hand, was quite pleased with the result. In the confusion no one noticed that I had opened the bidding rather light.

Hand 3

THE KIBITZER

A GOOD RULE FOR A KIBITZER to follow when watching a bridge game is to look at only one hand. But few kibitzers are this polite.

Playing rubber bridge, I pick up one of my usual:

♠ 87532   ♡ J8642   ◇ 76   ♣ 2

Both sides are vulnerable. While I'm reflecting to myself what a fine hand I'd have without the jack of hearts, the kibitzer loses interest in my hand and shifts his attention to North, my right hand opponent. I already know that I have a poor hand. Now everyone else knows also.

North opens the bidding with Two Clubs, strong and artificial. That's refreshing! With my partner and me passing throughout, the opponents bid Three No Trump on this auction:

NORTH	EAST	SOUTH	WEST
2♣	Pass	2♠	Pass
3♣	Pass	3◇	Pass
3♡	Pass	3NT	Pass
Pass	Pass		

Partner opens the deuce of diamonds. North puts down an impressive dummy:

NORTH
♠ A
♡ AKQ3
◇ AK
♣ K97543

                                        EAST
                                        ♠ 87532
                                        ♡ J8642
                                        ◇ 76
                                        ♣ 2

Prospects of setting Three No Trump are virtually nil. Oh well, at least my opponents haven't bid a slam.

The kibitzer, on his way to the kitchen to get a cup of coffee, takes a few seconds to inspect South's hand. (Two hands aren't enough; he has to see three.) The kibitzer then sends North a reassuring smile, shrugs his shoulders, and holds up four fingers. Wonderful! We can hold the hand to Four No-Trump.

Dummy's king of diamonds wins the first trick. Declarer cashes dummy's ace of spades and leads a club to his queen and partner's ace. Partner leads with second diamond to dummy's ace, which leaves:

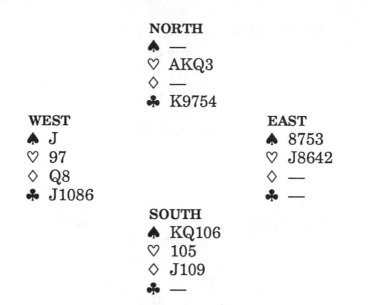

NORTH
♠ —
♡ AKQ3
◇ —
♣ K9754

WEST
♠ J
♡ 97
◇ Q8
♣ J1086

EAST
♠ 8753
♡ J8642
◇ —
♣ —

SOUTH
♠ KQ106
♡ 105
◇ J109
♣ —

Declarer cashes dummy's king of clubs, I pitch a spade and South discards a diamond. Now declarer cashes the ace, king and queen of hearts and exits with the three of hearts.

But I slip the deuce of hearts under the three, so dummy holds the lead. Partner, who is down to the queen of diamonds and the J-10-8 of clubs, wins the last four tricks, so we set Three No Trump one trick.

The complete hand:

                    NORTH
                    ♠ A
                    ♡ AKQ3
                    ◇ AK
                    ♣ K97543

WEST   **EAST**
♠ J9   ♠ 87532
♡ 97   ♡ J8642
◇ Q842   ◇ 76
♣ AJ1086   ♣ 2

                    SOUTH
                    ♠ KQ1064
                    ♡ 105
                    ◇ J10953
                    ♣ Q

One should never relax at a bridge game. It's easy to lose interest when holding poor cards. But on many hands a momentary lapse can prove fatal.

If East wins the fourth round of hearts, he can cash another heart, but he must lead a spade and South will win the last three tricks.

□   □   □

"You set Three No Trump?" asked the kibitzer upon returning from the kitchen. In order to satisfy the kibitzer's disbelief, we were forced to interrupt the bidding on the next hand, to review the play for him.

"You don't mind if I watch you again, do you?" asked the kibitzer.

"Of course not," I replied, "It's always a pleasure."

Hand 4

THE LIFE MASTER

TOURNAMENT PLAYERS in the U.S. are ranked according to the number of masterpoints they have accumulated. At the bottom of the list are the Junior Masters, players who have won 1 to 19 masterpoints, and the Masters, players who have won 20 to 49 masterpoints. Intermediate are the National Masters, Senior Masters, and Advanced Senior Masters with 50 to 99, 100 to 199, and 200 to 299, respectively. Finally at the top of the list are the Life Masters, players who have achieved their august rank by winning 300 or more masterpoints.

Playing in the Master's Pairs of a Regional Tournament, an event restricted to Life Masters, I pick the following hand in the West position:

♠ QJ107 ♡ K62 ◊ AQ4 ♣ J98

South, on my right, announces a skip bid of Four Hearts. I take the usual ten seconds and then pass. North and East also pass.

The bidding has been brief:

NORTH	EAST	SOUTH	WEST
—	—	4♡	Pass
Pass	Pass		

I lead the queen of spades. North puts down this dummy:

NORTH
♠ 8654
♡ 95
◊ K1063
♣ AQ4

WEST
♠ QJ107
♡ K62
◊ AQ4
♣ J98

South wins the opening lead with the ace of spades. He then cashes the king of clubs and the dummy's ace and queen of clubs, pitching a spade from hand. Dummy's nine of hearts is run for a finesse, losing to my king. I try a second spade, but declarer ruffs. Declarer then draws two more rounds of trumps, partner showing void, South having started with a seven card suit.

Since South has shown a doubleton spade and a doubleton club, its easy to count his original distribution as being 2-7-2-2. South leads another trump. There's nothing left to play of the hand but for the declarer to lead a diamond to dummy's king. but some people enjoy prolonging the play of the hand. As for me, I get my kicks pitching high cards, so I let go of the queen of diamonds not realizing what effect this would have on poor South.

The position now is:

NORTH
♠ 8
♡ —
◇ K106
♣ —

WEST
♠ 107
♡ —
◇ A4
♣ —

EAST
♠ K
♡ —
◇ J87
♣ —

SOUTH
♠ —
♡ 74
◇ 95
♣ —

South cashes another trump before leading a diamond. On the diamond lead, I play low and declarer finesses the ten. Partner wins the jack of diamonds, so we hold declarer to ten tricks for what should be an excellent match point score.

This was the full deal:

```
                    NORTH
                    ♠ 8654
                    ♡ 95
                    ◇ K1063
                    ♣ AQ4
  WEST                              EAST
  ♠ QJ107                          ♠ K92
  ♡ K62                            ♡ 3
  ◇ AQ4                            ◇ J872
  ♣ J98                            ♣ 107632
                    SOUTH
                    ♠ A3
                    ♡ AQJ10874
                    ◇ 95
                    ♣ K5
```

The masterpoint system of ranking players fails by measuring prolonged endeavor rather than relative skill. If masterpoints were a proper measure of skill then, in theory at least, anyone with a greater number of master points would have greater skill than a player with less masterpoints.

But what a fantastic commercial success masterpoints are! Where else but in the bridge world can one sell a nonexistent commodity at such inflated prices?

For want of a better name, I've dubbed the jettison of the queen of diamonds an Idiot Coup. Another Idiot Coup which I successfully executed at a recent duplicate, also against a Life Master, was the following:

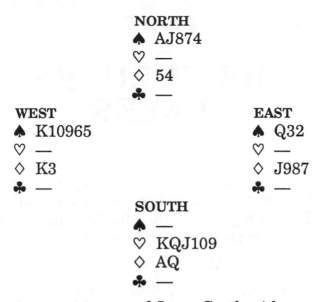

NORTH
♠ AJ874
♡ —
◇ 54
♣ —

WEST
♠ K10965
♡ —
◇ K3
♣ —

EAST
♠ Q32
♡ —
◇ J987
♣ —

SOUTH
♠ —
♡ KQJ109
◇ AQ
♣ —

Hearts were trump and I was South with no entry to the dummy. I raced off three round of trump, pitching the ace of spades from the dummy on the third round. On the fourth round, West came down to the king of spades and the doubleton king of diamonds. The lead of the last heart "squeezed" poor West. Forced to make a discard, he guessed wrong, pitching a diamond.

THE UNLUCKY PLAYER

MY PARTNER THIS RUBBER has been complaining all night about the poor cards that he has been holding and the bad breaks he's been getting. Thus far, he's had no one but himself to blame for his misfortunes.

Playing East I hold:

♠ Q83   ♡ 9   ◇ Q986   ♣ AKJ94

Both sides are vulnerable. South, on my left, opens one heart. Partner frowns and moans a pass. North raises to Two Hearts and South bids game.

The bidding has been:

NORTH	EAST	SOUTH	WEST
—	—	1♡	Pass
2♡	Pass	4♡	Pass
Pass	Pass		

Partner leads the deuce of clubs. North puts down an anemic raise:

NORTH
♠ K42
♡ 75432
◇ 754
♣ 83

EAST
♠ Q83
♡ 9
◇ Q986
♣ AKJ94

I win the king and ace of clubs and South drops the queen. South bids only five card majors, so his distribution ought to be 3-5-3-2, 4-5-2-2, or 2-5-4-2.

I don't see any need to lead a diamond now. If we have two tricks coming in diamonds, we'll always get them. And declarer may be short of entries to the dummy. I'd just as soon let South play the diamonds himself, so I return a trump.

Declarer wins the ace and king of hearts and partner drops the queen. South continues by leading the six of hearts to dummy's seven.

When declarer leads a diamond to his jack, I play the nine to show four, but partner wins the ace anyway and returns a diamond. South's diamonds are the K-J-10 and with the spade finesse working, he makes his contract.

The complete hand:

NORTH
♠ K42
♡ 75432
♢ 754
♣ 83

WEST
♠ 10965
♡ Q8
♢ A32
♣ 10752

EAST
♠ Q83
♡ 9
♢ Q986
♣ AKJ94

SOUTH
♠ AJ7
♡ AKJ106
♢ KJ10
♣ Q6

There's no use in telling partner that he could have set the hand by holding up his ace of diamonds. He's upset enough already. (If West lets the jack of diamonds hold, declarer enters dummy with the king of spades to repeat the diamond finesse. West wins the ace and exits with a diamond, leaving South stranded in hand with the ace-jack of spades and high hearts.)

South claims a hundred honors and partner exclaims, "I've never seen such a lucky hand. Two finesses and a trump break. Everything works against me. How long can a player continue to be this unlucky?"

Unlucky indeed! West was lucky that he didn't have a violent partner. North and South were lucky to make a game that could have been set. In fact, there was only one unlucky player at the table.

Hand 6

A FUN HAND

PLAYING RUBBER BRIDGE AGAINST AVERAGE OPPONENTS, I hold as South:

♠ 75   ♡ KQ10972   ◇ A7652   ♣ —

West, on my left, opens the bidding with Two Spades, weak. North overcalls Three Clubs, East bellows a loud Double, showing that he is well fixed in clubs, and it is my bid. Partner's Three Club overcall shows an opening hand or better. Partner probably has six clubs and three spades. His distribution may well be 3-1-3-6 or 3-2-2-6.

My heart spots are good enough to play opposite a singleton. Since I have a powerful playing hand, I bid Four Hearts, which all pass.

The bidding has been:

NORTH	EAST	SOUTH	WEST
—	—	—	2♠
3♣	Double	4♡	Pass
Pass	Pass		

West leads the deuce of clubs and North puts down this dummy:

19

NORTH
♠ A64
♡ 8
♦ 943
♣ AKQ873

SOUTH
♠ 75
♡ KQ10972
♦ A7652
♣ —

West's deuce of clubs is an obvious singleton. I win dummy's queen of clubs, pitching a spade from hand. I then play a heart to my ten, which holds, and continue with the king of hearts to East's ace.

On the second heart West follows with the six, which suggests that he holds a doubleton heart. If so, West's distribution ought to be 6-2-4-1, which gives East a distribution of 2-4-1-6.

East returns the jack of spades, which I win in dummy with the ace. I could cash dummy's two high clubs now, pitching diamonds from hand. But that would give me only nine tricks.

Instead, I ruff a spade with the seven of hearts, to remove East's last spade. This appears to leave me with no entry to dummy's high clubs. However, ruffing a spade was necessary, as I shall soon demonstrate.

I cash the queen of hearts. West, as expected, shows void.

I then play the ace of diamonds, to strip East of his singleton diamond. This is the position when I lead a heart to East's jack:

                         NORTH
                         ♠ —
                         ♡ —
                         ◇ 9
                         ♣ AK873
        WEST   EAST
        ♠ KQ9   ♠ —
        ♡ —   ♡ J
        ◇ KJ10   ◇ —
        ♣ —   ♣ J10965
                         SOUTH
                         ♠ —
                         ♡ 92
                         ◇ 7652
                         ♣ —

East, having nothing but clubs left, is forced to return the jack of clubs into the dummy's A-K-8-7-3. I sluff a diamond from hand and win the king in dummy. I return the seven of clubs to East's nine, again sluffing a diamond from hand. This leaves East on play with the 10-6-5 of clubs to lead into dummy's A-8-3. I win dummy's ace and eight of clubs, pitching another two diamonds from hand, so I make Four Hearts.

The complete hand:

                        NORTH
                        ♠ A64
                        ♡ 8
                        ◊ 943
                        ♣ AKQ873

    WEST   **EAST**
    ♠ KQ9832   ♠ J10
    ♡ 64   ♡ AJ53
    ◊ KJ108   ◊ Q
    ♣ 2   ♣ J109654

                        SOUTH
                        ♠ 75
                        ♡ KQ10972
                        ◊ A7652
                        ♣ —

Poor East suffers intolerably as he is endplayed to lead into dummy's clubs. I, on the other hand, enjoy this unusual endplay. For me, it was a fun hand.

22

Hand 7

THE PUPIL

I ALWAYS ENJOY PLAYING BRIDGE WITH A PUPIL. Rather than being upset with their lack of skill, I seem to find their innocence enchanting. And the plays they make and the questions they ask at the bridge table really make the day for me.

Playing in the Open Pairs of a Sectional Tournament with a novice, I hold:

♠ KJ10975   ♡ 8   ◇ J4   ♣ KQJ6

We are vulnerable and they are not. With a distribution of 6-4-2-1 and a good playing hand, I'm probably too good for a weak two bid. However, the alternatives, One Spade or Pass, don't appeal to me; so I open the bidding with Two Spades. West hesitates the full ten seconds and then some. Eventually, West passes. No doubt he is well fixed in his high cards. North passes and so does East, so Two Spades becomes the contract on this auction:

NORTH	EAST	SOUTH	WEST
—	—	2♠	Pass
Pass	Pass		

23

West leads the three of diamonds and North displays:

NORTH
♠ Q2
♡ A10642
◇ Q65
♣ 1095

SOUTH
♠ KJ10975
♡ 8
◇ J4
♣ KQJ6

Since a pitch on the third round of diamonds won't help me, I play dummy's queen on the opening lead. I'd just as soon have the opponents play three rounds of diamonds. But East has other plans. After winning the ace of diamonds he shifts to the eight of clubs. I play low and West wins the ace of clubs and returns a club which I win in hand.

I lead a spade to dummy's queen, which holds. When I continue with a spade to my jack, West wins the ace. Then he goes into a long huddle. Eventually, he leads a low diamond, trying to put East on lead for a club ruff. But I win the jack of diamonds, not East, so I make two overtricks.

The complete hand:

NORTH
- ♠ Q2
- ♡ A10642
- ♢ Q65
- ♣ 1095

WEST
- ♠ A63
- ♡ K953
- ♢ K1073
- ♣ A2

EAST
- ♠ 84
- ♡ QJ7
- ♢ A982
- ♣ 8743

SOUTH
- ♠ KJ10975
- ♡ 8
- ♢ J4
- ♣ KQJ6

It's often a good idea to play the queen with a holding of Q-x-x opposite J-x and also with Q-x-x opposite a small doubleton. And it's certainly correct to play the queen with Q-x opposite J-x or x-x.

Suppose the diamonds had been:

NORTH

◇ Q65

WEST

◇ K1073

EAST

◇ AJ82

SOUTH

◇ 94

If dummy plays low on the first diamond, East will win the jack. Later, when West wins the ace of spades, it will be easy for him to lead a diamond to his partner's ace for a club ruff. However, by playing the queen of diamonds declarer makes it difficult for West to lead a diamond and thus, declarer may avert a club ruff.

□   □   □

At the end of the hand partner asked, "Should I have bid more? Was it my fault we missed a game?"

"No," I replied, trying to keep a straight face. "You were right to pass. We were lucky to make Four Spades."

Hand 8

THE NIGHT PEOPLE

BEING ONE OF THE NIGHT PEOPLE, I'm quite used to keeping Dracula's hours. Thus you should not be surprised, dear reader, when I tell you the following hand was played at 3:00 a.m.

At such late hours it's tough enough to stay awake, let alone play a good game of bridge. But there are others who, like me, enjoy keeping unusual hours. They too face the difficult task of playing well after many hours of play.

Sitting East, I hold:

♠ 8   ♡ 42   ◇ AQJ9853   ♣ K93

Partner passes, North passes and I open the bidding with Three Diamonds, South overcalls Three Spades, West passes, and North raises to Four Spades, which all pass.

The bidding has been:

NORTH	EAST	SOUTH	WEST
—	—	—	Pass
Pass	3◇	3♠	Pass
4♠	Pass	Pass	Pass

Partner leads the ten of diamonds. North puts down this dummy:

NORTH
♠ Q653
♡ AQJ875
♢ 2
♣ Q4

EAST
♠ 8
♡ 42
♢ AQJ9853
♣ K93

The sight of the dummy is most discouraging. Obviously, we have no chance to set Four Spades. Or do we?

Apparently, the most amount of tricks the defense can hope to win is a diamond and two clubs. And that assumes that partner holds the ace of clubs. But if partner the ace of clubs, then South surely must hold the ace-king of spades and the king of hearts for his Three Spade overcall and we couldn't hope to win another trick.

Wait a minute! There's a chance to win another trick. If partner holds the J-x-x of spades, I may be able to "promote" a trump trick for him. At trick two, therefore, I return the king of clubs. This gives declarer a difficult guess after the ace and a third club from West.

This was the complete hand:

```
                    NORTH
                    ♠ Q653
                    ♡ AQJ875
                    ◇ 2
                    ♣ Q4
WEST                                    EAST
♠ J72                                   ♠ 8
♡ 10963                                 ♡ 42
◇ 104                                   ◇ AQJ9853
♣ A652                                  ♣ K93
                    SOUTH
                    ♠ AK1094
                    ♡ K
                    ◇ K76
                    ♣ J1087
```

In actual play, declarer believed that I held a doubleton king of clubs and ruffed the third club high in dummy. Down one!

THE MENTAL MIDGET

ONE OF THE PLAYERS in my rubber bridge game is a mental midget. He's gone down in two cold games and let me make a game that could have been set. Now it's my turn to play with him.

Sitting East, I hold:

♠ QJ5   ♡ Q109   ◇ A64   ♣ A863

Our opponents bid to Four Spades on this auction:

NORTH	EAST	SOUTH	WEST
—	—	1♣	Pass
1♡	Pass	1♠	Pass
3♡	Pass	3♠	Pass
4♠	Pass	Pass	Pass

Partner leads the jack of diamonds and North puts down this dummy:

NORTH
♠ K63
♡ AK87653
◇ 53
♣ 5

EAST
♠ QJ5
♡ Q109
◇ A64
♣ A863

I win the ace of diamonds and South drops the queen. South appears to hold the king-queen of diamonds doubleton. In view of the bidding and the play to date, South's most likely distribution is five spades, five clubs, two diamonds and therefore, a singleton heart.

South surely holds the ace of spades, the king-queen of diamonds and at least the queen-jack of clubs in high cards.

I see the defense winning a club, a diamond and a spade trick. Where are we going to get a fourth trick?

I could return a diamond at this point, which is a safe return that cannot cost a trick. But if I were to return a diamond, declarer would win the king of diamonds, play the ace of hearts and ruff a heart and then continue with the ace and king of spades. With both spades and hearts breaking three-two, dummy's hearts would be high and declarer would be able to run the hearts from dummy, making Four Spades.

In order to set Four Spades, it will be necessary to make dummy ruff a club, to remove the entry to dummy's hearts. To set Four Spades, I must find partner with king or queen of clubs. At trick two therefore, I underlead my ace of clubs. If partner wins the club and returns a club, declarer will be forced to ruff in dummy or let me win the ace of clubs. With this defense, Four Spades can be set.

The complete hand:

NORTH
♠ K63
♡ AK87653
♢ 53
♣ 5

WEST
♠ 92
♡ 42
♢ J109872
♣ K42

EAST
♠ QJ5
♡ Q109
♢ A64
♣ A863

SOUTH
♠ A10874
♡ J
♢ KQ
♣ QJ1097

Unfortunately, the defense did not proceed as I had planned. Partner won the king of clubs and returned a diamond to South's king. Declarer continued with the ace of hearts and a heart ruff, followed by the ace of spades and a spade to dummy's king. Dummy's heart's were now high, so declarer made Four Spades.

"Why didn't you return a club?" I asked. "Couldn't you see that I was trying to make dummy ruff a club?"

"How should I know," responded the Mental Midget. "Declarer's first bid suit was clubs and I was afraid if I returned a club that dummy would pitch a losing diamond."

At this point, I felt like strangling my partner. Instead, I attempted to humiliate him by challenging him to a set game at 10¢ per point.

"To make it fair, I'll let you pick your partner and my partner," I said.

"I accept," said the Mental Midget. " I choose Meyer Schleiffer as my partner." Meyer is one of the all-time great bridge players who has won numerous National titles and has represented the United States in world competition play. He is a formidable foe to be playing against in any bridge game.

"And who do you pick as my partner?" I asked, confident that no matter who was chosen for me I would have the best of it.

"Give me some time to think about it," he responded.

Days went by and then weeks. Whenever I asked the Mental Midget to select a partner for me and play the promised set match, he always responded that he needed more time to consider the matter.

"Coward!" I said.

Finally, many months later, one of the elderly players at our bridge club suffered a stroke and paramedics were summoned to transport him to the hospital.

"That's him," said the Mental Midget, pointing to the man on the stretcher, "That's your partner."

Hand 10

BIRTHDAY PRESENT

TOMORROW IS MY GIRL FRIEND'S BIRTHDAY. It looks as though I can afford to buy her a nice present, for my partner has just opened the bidding with One No Trump and I hold:

♠ K9   ♡ AQ754   ◊ AJ1093   ♣ 2

I jump to Three Hearts and partner raises me to Four Hearts. I could bid Six Hearts now, but instead I offer partner an alternative with Six Diamonds. Over Six Diamonds partner does the unexpected; he raises me to Seven Diamonds.

The bidding has been:

NORTH	EAST	SOUTH	WEST
1NT	Pass	3♡	Pass
4♡	Pass	6◊	Pass
7◊	Pass	Pass	Pass

West leads the three of spades. Commenting that he must have the perfect hand for me, partner puts down:

NORTH

♠ A2
♡ K32
◇ KQ2
♣ AJ863

SOUTH

♠ K9
♡ AQ754
◇ AJ1093
♣ 2

Yes indeed, partner does have an ideal hand for me. Barring a bad heart split, we will make a vulnerable grand slam!

Is there anything I can do if the hearts break 4-1? There are two lines of play. I can cash two rounds of trump and then attempt to ruff a heart in the dummy. Or I can play to ruff three clubs in hand. Then if the trumps break 3-2 and the clubs divide 4-3, I can set up the fifth club and I won't need more than three top hearts.

Which is the better line? Let's see. West led a low spade. That suggests that the spades are divided 5-4. Assuming that the hand with five spades will hold the singleton heart, I would need an opponent to hold a distribution of 5-1-2-5 to be able to ruff the fourth round of hearts in dummy. Alternatively, the dummy reversal would succeed against a distribution of 5-1-3-4. I make the second distribution more likely, so I plan to ruff three clubs in hand.

I win the first spade in hand and cash the jack of diamonds. When everyone follows it becomes safe to ruff a club, so I lead a club to dummy's ace and ruff a club. Then I lead a trump to dummy's queen. If the trumps divide 4-1, I'll have to rely on a 3-2 heart split. But both opponents follow to the second round of trumps so I continue by ruffing another club to hand.

It must be right to lead a heart to the dummy rather than a spade, for when I ruff the fourth round of clubs, I don't want an opponent to be able to pitch a singleton heart. After a club ruff and a spade to dummy's ace, I cash dummy's high trump and claim thirteen tricks.

My precautions were necessary, for this was the complete hand:

```
                    NORTH
                    ♠ A2
                    ♡ K32
                    ◇ KQ2
                    ♣ AJ863
    WEST                            EAST
    ♠ 1043                          ♠ QJ8765
    ♡ J1086                         ♡ 9
    ◇ 54                            ◇ 876
    ♣ K1097                         ♣ Q54
                    SOUTH
                    ♠ K9
                    ♡ AQ754
                    ◇ AJ1093
                    ♣ 2
```

If declarer enters dummy with the ace of spades in order to ruff the fourth round of clubs, East pitches his singleton heart.

Hand 11

A DEEP FINESSE

PLAYING SOUTH IN A RUBBER BRIDGE GAME, I deal myself the following hand:

♠ A9   ♡ KJ109742   ◇ AQ85   ♣ —

I open the bidding with One Heart. West overcalls Five Clubs, North and East pass and it is my bid. It's possible that the opponents may be able to make Five Clubs. It's also possible that we can make Five Hearts if, for instance, partner holds the queen of hearts and five diamonds. In any event, I'm not about to let the opponents play Five Clubs, so I bid Five Hearts. West doubles and all pass.

The bidding has been:

NORTH	EAST	SOUTH	WEST
—	—	1♡	5♣
Pass	Pass	5♡	Double
Pass	Pass	Pass	

West leads the king of clubs and North puts down this suitable dummy:

NORTH
♠ 875
♡ Q86
◇ K743
♣ 876

SOUTH
♠ A9
♡ KJ109742
◇ AQ85
♣ —

Five Hearts is cold if the diamonds split three-two. However, in view of West's Five Club bid, the diamonds may well be breaking four-one, with West holding a singleton. In any event, I need to discover how the spades lie, so I ruff the opening club lead and play the ace and nine of spades.

West wins the second spade with the jack and continues with another club. I ruff in hand and lead a trump. West wins the ace of hearts and exits with a heart which I win in dummy with the eight, East pitching a spade. I ruff a spade to hand, West following with the king.

It's time now to count West's hand. West was dealt three spades and two hearts. He has one of the two following hands:

1. ♠ KJx   ♡ Ax   ◇ xx   ♣ AKQJxx

2. ♠ KJx   ♡ Ax   ◇ x   ♣ AKQJxxx

I'm sure that West holds seven clubs, rather than six, for his Five Club bid, which leaves him with a singleton diamond. I hope that his singleton is a jack, ten or nine. Sure enough, this is the position when I lead a diamond to dummy's king:

```
                    NORTH
                    ♠  —
                    ♡  Q
                    ◇  K743
                    ♣  8
        WEST                            EAST
        ♠  —                            ♠  Q
        ♡  —                            ♡  —
        ◇  10                           ◇  J962
        ♣  AQJ9                         ♣  10
                    SOUTH
                    ♠  —
                    ♡  KJ
                    ◇  AQ85
                    ♣  —
```

West plays the ten of diamonds under dummy's king. On the return I finesse the eight of diamonds, playing East for an original holding of J-9-x-x of diamonds. The eight of diamonds holds, so I make Five Hearts, doubled.

The complete hand:

```
                    NORTH
                    ♠  875
                    ♡  Q86
                    ◇  K743
                    ♣  876
        WEST                            EAST
        ♠  KJ4                          ♠  Q10632
        ♡  A5                           ♡  3
        ◇  10                           ◇  J962
        ♣  AKQJ952                      ♣  1043
                    SOUTH
                    ♠  A9
                    ♡  KJ109742
                    ◇  AQ85
                    ♣  —
```

39

Hand 12

PIPPING
THE OPPONENTS

WHEN PLAYING IN A FOUR DEAL GAME, it pays to watch the score on the fourth deal. On the fourth deal I hold as South:

♠ QJ1083   ♡ 5   ◇ A72   ♣ AKQ2

Both sides are vulnerable and I am the dealer. I open the bidding with One Spade. West overcalls Two Hearts and North raises me to Two Spades. East passes and I bid Four Spades, which all pass.

The bidding has been:

NORTH	EAST	SOUTH	WEST
—	—	1♠	2♡
2♠	Pass	4♠	Pass
Pass	Pass		

West leads the queen of hearts and partner puts down this hand:

NORTH
♠ K94
♡ A94
♢ J65
♣ J965

SOUTH
♠ QJ1083
♡ 5
♢ A72
♣ AKQ2

I win the ace of hearts and East drops the eight. When I lead a spade to my queen, West wins the ace and plays the jack of hearts, which I ruff. I cash two more rounds of trump, West pitching a heart on the third round.

I have ten top tricks. Before claiming game, I check the score. Thus far things have been rather even our opponents have scored 100 and 420 and we have scored 420. If I settle for four spades, we will be ahead 1040 to 520, for a net 520 or five points. But making five spades would "pip" the opponents 1070 to 520, for a net win of six points.

The hand looks simple. I can cash ten tricks, but no more. Is there any chance at all of making an overtrick? There's no play for a squeeze. What about an endplay? That's a possibility. In fact, if West holds the king-queen of diamonds, I think I have him no matter how he defends.

The hearts appear to be divided five-four. When I play off three top clubs West pitches a diamond. Since West started with two clubs and two spades, I place him with an original distribution of 2-5-4-2. The following cards are left:

41

```
                    NORTH
                    ♠ —
                    ♡ 9
                    ◇ J65
                    ♣ J
      WEST                          EAST
      ♠ —                           ♠ —
      ♡ 107                         ♡ K6
      ◇ KQ8                         ◇ 1094
      ♣ —                           ♣ —
                    SOUTH
                    ♠ 8
                    ♡ —
                    ◇ A72
                    ♣ 2
```

On the lead of a club to the jack West pitches a heart. I ruff a heart to hand, which reduces West to three diamonds.

As there is only one heart left in play, I can safely lead a diamond toward dummy's jack. West wins with the king and returns a low diamond. I rise with dummy's jack of diamonds, which holds, so I make five spades.

The complete hand:

                        NORTH
                        ♠ K94
                        ♡ A94
                        ◇ J65
                        ♣ J965

WEST   **EAST**
♠ A5   ♠ 762
♡ QJ1072   ♡ K863
◇ KQ83   ◇ 1094
♣ 108   ♣ 743

                        SOUTH
                        ♠ QJ1083
                        ♡ 5
                        ◇ A72
                        ♣ AKQ2

The difficult part of the hand was to conceive the endplay. Once declarer decides to play West for the king-queen of diamonds, he must come to eleven tricks.

Hand 13

THE MOMENT OF TRUTH

WHILE PLAYING IN THE KNOCKOUT TEAMS at a National Tournament, I pick up the following hand as South:

♠ AK7   ♡ AQJ104   ◊ 83   ♣ 1097

East, on my right, opens the bidding with One Spade and I overcall Two Hearts. West passes and partner raises me to Four Hearts, which all pass.

The bidding has been:

NORTH	EAST	SOUTH	WEST
—	1♠	2♡	Pass
4♡	Pass	Pass	Pass

West leads the deuce of spades and North puts down this dummy:

NORTH
♠ 43
♡ 9865
◊ K4
♣ AQJ83

SOUTH
♠ AK7
♡ AQJ104
◊ 83
♣ 1097

44

East plays the queen of spades which I win with the ace. East obviously holds the majority of the missing high cards. It looks right, therefore, to continue with the king of spades and a spade ruff to dummy, followed by a heart finesse. If East holds the king of hearts, then I can make eleven tricks.

But West may hold the king of hearts. If so, West will win the heart finesse and shift to a diamond and I will lose a heart, two diamonds and a club, for down one.

Can I make Four Hearts if West holds the king of hearts? I suppose I could play the ace of hearts to guard against West holding the singleton king. But that wouldn't work, for if East has opened the bidding without the king of hearts, then East surely has a singleton heart and West would hold K-x-x.

I wonder if anything might be gained by leading the queen of hearts from hand. It's IMP scoring, so I can afford to lose an extra trick to East if he holds the king of hearts.

Let's see. If East wins the king of hearts, then West will never gain the lead and I will lose at most a heart, a diamond, and a club. On the other hand, if West happens to hold the king of hearts and ducks the first heart, then I may be able to pitch one of my diamonds on dummy's clubs before West can gain the lead. Yes, leading the queen of hearts must be the correct play, for it gives me some chance of making Four Hearts when West holds the king of hearts.

West studies the queen of hearts for a few seconds. This is the moment of truth. If West plays his king of hearts, then he'll surely shift to diamond and I'll be down one. West, however, fearful that East might hold a singleton ace of hearts, ducks my queen of hearts. North and East follow low. I continue with the ace of hearts. East shows void, pitching the ten of diamonds.

45

I try the club finesse, losing to East's king. Fortunately, West has three clubs, so I am able to pitch one of my losing diamonds on dummy's clubs before West can ruff in, making Four Hearts.

This was the complete hand:

NORTH
♠ 43
♡ 9865
◇ K4
♣ AQJ83

WEST
♠ J92
♡ K72
◇ 9752
♣ 652

EAST
♠ Q10865
♡ 3
◇ AQJ106
♣ K4

SOUTH
♠ AK7
♡ AQJ104
◇ 83
♣ 1097

Since East's diamonds are much stronger than his spades, East should give some consideration to opening the bidding with One Diamond rather than One Spade. As it happens, a diamond lead from West will set Four Hearts.

Hand 14

A GERIATRIC ADVENTURE

THIS HAND COMES FROM THE MAYFAIR BRIDGE CLUB in New York City in 1965, where the late Harry Fishbein, who always treated me well, has asked me to pick up a hand for him in one of the half-cent games. So, instead of playing with my peers in a nickel-a-point game, I find myself playing in a game that consists of three little old ladies and me.

Sitting West I hold:

♠ 5   ♡ AJ10842   ◇ J54   ♣ AQ2

North, on my left, Passes and partner Passes. South, on my right, opens the bidding with One Diamond. Partner and I haven't discussed our jump overcalls. No matter. I overcall Two Hearts. North bids an enthusiatic Two Spades and partner passes. North-South eventually reach Five Diamonds on this auction:

NORTH	EAST	SOUTH	WEST
Pass	Pass	1◇	2♡
2♠	Pass	3◇	Pass
4◇	Pass	5◇	Pass
Pass	Pass		

Not wanting to lead a from my tenaces in hearts and clubs, I chose to lead my singleton spade. Most likely the spades divided 5-5-2-1 around the table and a spade lead will not cost a trick.

North puts down this dummy:

NORTH
♠ AQ962
♡ 76
◇ KQ
♣ J983

WEST
♠ 5
♡ AJ10842
◇ J54
♣ AQ2

Dummy ducks the opening spade lead, partner plays the seven of spades and declarer wins with the king. South leads a diamond to dummy's king and queen. On the second diamond partner plays a low club, declarer having started with seven trumps. After some thought, declarer leads a heart from dummy, partner plays the nine, declarer the king and I win the ace.

It's time now to count the hand. South has shown with seven diamonds. Since she didn't attempt to pitch on dummy's ace-queen of spades, declarer certainly holds two spades. Partner's play of the nine of hearts suggests a doubleton, which gives South the king-queen third. South's distribution, therefore ought to be 2-3-7-1.

I could return the jack of hearts at this point, which is a safe return that cannot cost a trick. But a heart return would allow declarer to pull my last trump, winning seven diamonds, one heart and three spades, for a total of eleven tricks.

No, a heart return won't do. To set Five Diamonds, I must underlead the ace-queen of clubs to partner's king, in order to get a spade ruff.

The complete hand:

NORTH
- ♠ AQ962
- ♡ 76
- ◇ KQ
- ♣ J983

WEST
- ♠ 5
- ♡ AJ10842
- ◇ J54
- ♣ AQ2

EAST
- ♠ J10873
- ♡ 95
- ◇ 2
- ♣ K7654

SOUTH
- ♠ K4
- ♡ KQ3
- ◇ A1098763
- ♣ 10

This hand had a happy ending for declarer. After winning the king of clubs, partner returned a heart! Declarer won the queen of hearts, pulled my last trump, and discarded her heart loser on dummy's spades, making Five Diamonds.

Normally, I don't say anything when my partner misdefends a hand. But on this occasion, I couldn't resist directing an inquiry to East.

"Listen," I said, "When your partner underleads his ace-queen of clubs to your king, don't you think there's some reason for the play? Couldn't you have guessed to return a spade for me to ruff?"

"Oh!" she replied, "Are you my partner?"

49

Hand 15

THE GOSSIPS

PLAYING IN THE OPEN PAIRS of a Sectional Tournament, I come up against two little old ladies. I know them well. They're both gossips. And today is another opportunity they can't resist. "You're a friend of Alan, aren't you?" asks the first little old lady.

"Yes, I am," I reply.

"Isn't that Alan's wife over there playing with Gary?" asks the second little old lady. "This is the second time they've played together."

"Yes, and I saw them together at Chasen's last Thursday," says the first Gossip. (This was a complete fabrication, but it added great flavor to the tale being told).

"They've been seeing each other secretly," says the second Gossip.

"Thanks for telling me ladies. I'll be sure to warn Alan about that Casanova Gary," I say. At this point both women smile. They have performed their duty as Gossips.

Now it's time to play bridge. I pick up:

♠ KQJ108   ♡ A   ◇ Q83   ♣ J1065

I open One Spade. West Passes and partner responds Three No-Trump. So far as I'm concerned, a Three No-Trump response to One Heart or One Spade ought to be reserved for a strong major raise rather than a balanced hand of 16 to 18 points. Too often the opening bidder will have an unbalanced hand and be forced to guess whether or not to bid again. This is one of those hands. It could be the wrong thing to do, but I'm going to bid Four Spades. All pass, so the bidding has been:

NORTH	EAST	SOUTH	WEST
—	—	1♠	Pass
3NT	Pass	4♠	Pass
Pass	Pass		

West leads the four of hearts. North puts down this dummy:

NORTH
♠ 965
♡ QJ7
◇ AKJ
♣ KQ82

SOUTH
♠ KQJ108
♡ A
◇ Q83
♣ J1065

I see we are in the best contract. If the spades and clubs break 3-2, I should have no trouble making five spades.

But the spades may be breaking 4-1. If so, then I can't afford to ruff two hearts; I may have to let West win the king of hearts if she has it.

I win the ace of hearts in hand and enter dummy with the with the ace of diamonds in order to lead a trump from dummy. If I can sneak a trump through East, then I can discover how the trumps are breaking before my opponents lead a second heart.

East plays low on the lead of a spade and my king wins the trick. On the second round however, West shows void, pitching a low heart, and East wins the ace. This is the position I anticipated earlier. If East returns a low heart now, I can't afford to ruff. I'll have to pitch a club and let West win the king of hearts.

East, however, is intent on obtaining a ruff and returns the three of clubs. West wins the ace and attempts to cash the king of hearts! I ruff and pull East's remaining trumps, making five spades.

This was the complete hand:

```
                    NORTH
                    ♠ 965
                    ♡ QJ7
                    ◇ AKJ
                    ♣ KQ82
     WEST                              EAST
     ♠ 2                               ♠ A743
     ♡ K8643                           ♡ 10952
     ◇ 654                             ◇ 10972
     ♣ A974                            ♣ 3
                    SOUTH
                    ♠ KQJ108
                    ♡ A
                    ◇ Q83
                    ♣ J1065
```

While East is berating her partner for failing to give her a club ruff it occurs to me that good defense should set Four Spades. East should return the deuce of hearts rather than a club. South must take a pitch. West then wins the king of hearts, cashes the ace of clubs and gives East a club ruff for down one!

□　　□　　□

"Look," says one of the gossips, referring to a local expert on his way to the men's room. "There he goes again, wandering about the room trying to cop a board."

The gossips in the bridge world are quite malicious. In truth, their perception of reality is no more acute than their bridge game.

Hand 16

THE CIGAR SMOKER

WHENEVER I PLAY DUPLICATE BRIDGE, I take one of the cardboard backs from my laundered shirts and write upon it "Please don't smoke". I try to sit North-South and I'm usually successful in persuading my opponents not to smoke for a round.

It's always harder to find courteous opponents when playing East-West. Somehow a traveling pair seems to lack status. There are always a few players who insist upon smoking in spite of my protests.

Playing against a cigar smoker, I pick up the following hand in the East position:

♠ J103 ♡ QJ109 ◇ KJ4 ♣ J97

Both sides are vulnerable. South, my left hand opponent, opens One Heart. Partner passes and North responds Two Clubs. I pass and the auction continues:

NORTH	EAST	SOUTH	WEST
—	—	1♡	Pass
2♣	Pass	4♡	Pass
Pass	Pass		

Partner leads the deuce of spades. North puts down:

NORTH
♠ 876
♡ 43
◇ AQ76
♣ AQ62

EAST
♠ J103
♡ QJ109
◇ KJ4
♣ J97

Declarer wins my ten of spades with the ace. After cashing the ace of hearts, declarer leads a diamond, partner plays the ten, dummy the queen, and I win the king.

Partner can't have underlead the king-queen of spades, so declarer is marked with the ace-king of spades. Partner's lead of the deuce of spades and his play of the ten of diamonds marks South with a likely distribution of 3-6-2-2.

Declarer is sure to win two spades, four trump tricks, a diamond and two clubs, nine tricks in all. Now, if I were to return a spade or a heart, then dummy would retain enough entries for South to make an extra trump trick by ruffing two diamonds and a club. The defense would be unable to prevent declarer from making the ace-king of hearts and three of his small trumps.

That is why I must return a club into dummy's ace-queen.

The complete hand:

```
                    NORTH
                    ♠ 876
                    ♡ 43
                    ◊ AQ76
                    ♣ AQ62
    WEST                            EAST
    ♠ Q942                          ♠ J103
    ♡ 2                             ♡ QJ109
    ◊ 10983                         ◊ KJ4
    ♣ K1085                         ♣ J97
                    SOUTH
                    ♠ AK5
                    ♡ AK8765
                    ◊ 52
                    ♣ 43
```

The club return takes out a vital entry. Declarer is able to make two of his small trumps ruffing, but not three. The defense eventually wins a diamond, a spade and two trump tricks, for down one.

If East returns a spade, South wins in hand, cashes the king of hearts, leads a diamond to the ace and ruffs a diamond. Declarer continues with a club to dummy's queen and another diamond ruff, followed by the ace of clubs and a club. This allows South to make an extra trump trick en-passant.

□   □   □

I took extra pleasure in setting this hand because South had refused to put out his cigar, which shows how easily many bridge players can be provoked. Imagine, here I was taking offense at a complete stranger just because he blew a little cigar smoke in my face.

A MIRACLE DISTRIBUTION

PLAYING RUBBER BRIDGE, I DEAL MYSELF:

♠ AK654   ♡ 74   ◇ AK82   ♣ K3

I open the bidding with One Spade. West passes and North raises me to Two Spades. East passes and I bid game. All pass, so the bidding has been:

NORTH	EAST	SOUTH	WEST
—	—	1♠	Pass
2♠	Pass	4♠	Pass
Pass	Pass		

West leads the king of hearts and North puts down this decent dummy:

NORTH
♠ 872
♡ A6
◇ Q103
♣ Q7654

SOUTH
♠ AK654
♡ 74
◇ AK82
♣ K3

Not bad at all! Four Spades is cold if the trumps break three-two, for after playing the ace and king of spades, I can ruff my losing diamond in dummy.

I win the opening lead with dummy's ace of hearts and cash the ace and king of spades, but East shows void on the king of spades.

That's a disappointment. It looks as though I must go down at least one in Four Spades, for I have two spades, a heart and a club to lose.

I could play three rounds of diamonds. Then if the diamonds broke three-three, I could pitch dummy's losing heart on the fourth diamond. But a three-three diamond split wouldn't help me, for West would ruff in, pull dummy's last trump and cash a high heart.

No, in order to make Four Spades, I need for West to follow to four rounds of diamonds so I can pitch dummy's heart and ruff a heart. Four Spades can be made only by finessing dummy's ten of diamonds, playing West for four diamonds to the jack.

Fortunately, West does in fact hold four diamonds to the jack, a miracle distribution, so I am able to pitch dummy's losing heart as West follows helplessly to the diamonds. Now I ruff my losing heart and concede a club and two spades making game.

The complete hand:

NORTH
♠ 872
♡ A6
◇ Q103
♣ Q7654

WEST
♠ QJ93
♡ KQ9
◇ J974
♣ J8

EAST
♠ 10
♡ J108532
◇ 65
♣ A1092

SOUTH
♠ AK654
♡ 74
◇ AK82
♣ K3

If you believe this story, you probably believe in the Tooth Fairy as well. Here's what really happens when declarer plays for a miracle distribution and finesses dummy's ten of diamonds:

NORTH
♠ 872
♡ A6
◇ Q103
♣ Q7654

WEST
♠ QJ93
♡ KQ93
◇ 974
♣ J8

EAST
♠ 10
♡ J10852
◇ J65
♣ A1092

SOUTH
♠ AK654
♡ 74
◇ AK82
♣ K3

East wins the jack of diamonds and returns a heart to West. West cashes the queen and jack of spades and continues with another heart. East saves all of his hearts and declarer never wins a club trick, so declarer goes down three on a hand that should have been held to down one.

In short, while miracle distributions occasionally do exist, enabling a resourceful declarer to make a contract that otherwise would be set, the cost of playing for miracles can be, and often is, a risk not worth taking.

Hand 18

THE NEEDLER

THE WEST PLAYER IN MY GAME IS A NEEDLER. All afternoon he's been gloating over his opponents. His brilliant
defense was the only way to set a hand; they let him make
a doubled game; they failed to bid a cold slam, etc. Oh, he's
a good player all right, but he seems to be more interested
in showing off than in winning. I wonder if he can take it
if things start breaking against him.

Playing rubber bridge, I hold as South:

♠ A3　♡ AK9　◇ 875　♣ Q9853

I open One Club. Partner responds One Diamond. I
rebid One No-Trump and partner raises me to Three
No-Trump, which all pass.

The bidding has been:

NORTH	EAST	SOUTH	WEST
—	—	1♣	Pass
1◇	Pass	1NT	Pass
3NT	Pass	Pass	Pass

West leads the two of spades. Partner puts down:

NORTH
♠ K7
♡ 832
◇ AQJ96
♣ A74

SOUTH
♠ A3
♡ AK9
◇ 875
♣ Q9853

Not bad at all! I should have no trouble making Three No-Trump unless East holds four diamonds king-ten.

Is there anything I can do if diamonds fail to produce four tricks? I suppose I could make some play in clubs. Four club tricks would be enough to make Three No-Trump. But the trouble is that I don't know that the diamonds are splitting badly. No, I can't afford to play clubs, surrendering the lead, when I'm an overwhelming favorite to bring home the diamonds.

I only have to worry when West has a singleton diamond. Assuming that West has a singleton diamond, then his distribution would easily be 4-1-4-4. (West led the deuce of spades; if West held five hearts, he might have chosen to lead a heart rather than a spade.) Hence, East might hold a singleton jack or ten of clubs.

In any event, it costs nothing to win the opening lead in hand and play the queen of clubs toward dummy's ace. It's a bluff play, of course, for if West fails to cover, I'll play dummy's ace of clubs and follow with the ace and queen of diamonds, making Three No-Trump unless East started with four diamonds king-ten.

But West does cover the queen of clubs with the king. I play dummy's ace and drops the jack! Now I force out the ten of clubs, making Three No-Trump without needing dummy's diamonds.

The complete hand:

```
                    NORTH
                    ♠ K7
                    ♡ 832
                    ◇ AQJ96
                    ♣ A74
    WEST                            EAST
    ♠ J962                          ♠ Q10854
    ♡ 10654                         ♡ QJ7
    ◇ 4                             ◇ K1032
    ♣ K1062                         ♣ J
                    SOUTH
                    ♠ A3
                    ♡ AK9
                    ◇ 875
                    ♣ Q9853
```

"You know, you could have set the hand if you had ducked the queen of clubs," I said to the needler. "I was going to play dummy's ace anyway."

"Yes, but....."

"Yes, but nothing. You misdefended the hand and you know it. You let me make a vulnerable game when I should have gone down two," I said.

"That's right," chimed North and East, each of whom had been the target of West's earlier sarcasms, "You misdefended the hand."

One thing a needler can't stand is to be made to look foolish. When the rubber was over, West suddenly remembered an important engagement he simply had to keep and left.

Hand 19

THE FRIENDLY MAN

WHY DO I PLAY DUPLICATE BRIDGE? It isn't for the glory. Nor do I have any interest in winning masterpoints. No, I play tournament bridge because it's a great social activity. I really enjoy playing bridge with my friends and I further enjoy making friends with other bridge players.

Playing in a Sectional Tournament against opponents whose play on the previous board has marked them as weak players, I hold as South:

♠ AQJ95   ♡ Q3   ◇ A75   ♣ 764

We are vulnerable and they are not. I am first to bid and open One Spade. West overcalls Two Hearts and North leaps to Four Spades. East passes, I pass and West, after considerable thought, also passes.

The bidding has been:

NORTH	EAST	SOUTH	WEST
—	—	1♠	2♡
4♠	Pass	Pass	Pass

West leads the five of clubs. North puts down this dummy:

NORTH
♠ K10874
♡ A75
◇ J843
♣ K

SOUTH
♠ AQJ95
♡ Q3
◇ A75
♣ 764

It's evident from dummy's good trumps that West was not contemplating a double of Four Spades. No doubt he was considering a save at favorable vulnerability.

East wins dummy's king of clubs with the ace and shifts to the ten of hearts. If I duck the heart, it's unlikely that East will switch and I'll have more time to decide how to play the diamonds. Good! East continues with another heart which I win in dummy with the ace.

I've already lost a club and a heart. somehow, I've got to avoid losing two diamonds as well. The best chance to make Four Spades is to lead a diamond to my ace. Then, if West has a doubleton king or queen and fails to unlock, I can pull trumps, strip out the clubs and hearts and play a second diamond. Against better opponents I would have to give some consideration in regard to the best time to play the ace of diamonds without prompting an unblock. But against this particular West defender I probably don't have to worry. He's not up to unblocking the king or queen of diamonds under my ace.

I ruff dummy's last heart, East following suit. When I ruff a club in the dummy, West plays the deuce. It was nice of West to count the clubs for me. I play two rounds of trump and West shows with a doubleton. West's distribution must be 2-5-1-5, so after ruffing my last club in dummy I duck a diamond to West, playing him for a singleton honor.

The complete hand:

```
                    NORTH
                    ♠ K10874
                    ♡ A75
                    ◇ J843
                    ♣ K
     WEST                            EAST
     ♠ 62                            ♠ 3
     ♡ KJ864                         ♡ 1092
     ◇ K                             ◇ Q10962
     ♣ Q10852                        ♣ AJ93
                    SOUTH
                    ♠ AQJ95
                    ♡ Q3
                    ◇ A75
                    ♣ 764
```

Even if West had not counted the clubs for declarer, South should still guess his distribution, for West would hardly have hesitated over Four Spades with:

♠ xx   ♡ KJxxx   ◇ Kx   ♣ Q10xx

It's a good point to remember. Hesitations do not go unnoticed by an observant declarer and indeed may assist him later in the play.

"Should I have taken the Five Club save?" West asks, addressing his question to me. Even though we were strangers, West was a Friendly Man and it was natural for him to talk to me. I took an immediate liking to him and I was glad to discuss the hand with him.

West and I became friends. Over the years, I continued to see him at local tournaments. Whenever we meet, he invariably comes over, shakes my hand, and said, "How have you been Jim? It's good to see you again."

Hand 20

THE HUNGRY MAN

THERE ARE ALL SORTS OF HUNGRY MEN in the bridge world. Most are content to chew on their pencils or munch on their cigars. A few prefer to nibble on their ties. And then there are those who feast on themselves.

Playing West in a sectional tournament, I come up against a man who has the habit of eating his fingernails down to the elbow. As West I hold:

♠ K53   ♡ Q1065   ◇ J1098   ♣ A2

Both sides are vulnerable and South, to my right, opens One Heart. I pass and North responds One Spade. With East-West silent throughout, our opponents bid game on this auction:

NORTH	EAST	SOUTH	WEST
—	—	1♡	Pass
1♠	Pass	3◇	Pass
3♠	Pass	3NT	Pass
Pass	Pass		

I lead the jack of diamonds. North puts down this dummy:

                    NORTH
                    ♠ AJ1086
                    ♡ 4
                    ◇ 63
                    ♣ QJ963
    WEST
    ♠ K53
    ♡ Q1065
    ◇ J1098
    ♣ A2

Partner, an expert player, plays the deuce of diamonds and South wins the ace. At the second trick South leads the king of clubs which I win with the ace, partner dropping the eight.

Partner's eight of clubs is for count, showing that he holds four clubs. That gives South a doubleton club. From the bidding, South's most likely distribution is 2-5-4-2.

Since partner played the deuce of diamonds on the first trick, I'm sure that South holds the A-K-Q of diamonds. Leading another diamond, then, would not set up any immediate winners for the defense. A club return must be best, for dummy's queen of clubs is the entry to the spade suit.

Declarer seems distressed when I return a club. Silence reigns except for a slight gnawing as South consumes one of his thumbs. After a mouthful, South returns to hand with a diamond. When he leads a spade to dummy's A-J-10, I put up the king and it's all over for declarer. Good play at this point would still bring home Three No-Trump, for a poor match point score. But in practice, after devouring the unexpired portion of his thumb, declarer goes down one when he ducks my king of spades and subsequently finesses the spades again.

The complete hand:

NORTH
♠ AJ1086
♡ 4
◊ 63
♣ QJ963

WEST
♠ K53
♡ Q1065
◊ J1098
♣ A2

EAST
♠ Q72
♡ 973
◊ 542
♣ 10874

SOUTH
♠ 94
♡ AKJ82
◊ AKQ7
♣ K5

If West fails to return a club after winning the ace, then declarer will have no trouble making eleven tricks, for the queen of clubs is the entry to dummy's spades.

Hand 21

THE JERK

I MAKE MANY UNUSUAL PLAYS AT THE BRIDGE TABLE. Not all of them turn out well. But I've learned to accept my misfortunes with a smile, for that's part of the game.

Playing in a four deal game, I deal myself the following hand on the second deal:

♠ 973   ♡ —   ♢ KQJ986   ♣ Q1098

We are vulnerable and they are not. With a void, this is hardly an ideal hand for a weak two bid, but to my mind it's better to enter an auction early rather than to pass and compete later. At rubber bridge especially, it pays to bid at low levels, so I open the bidding with Two Diamonds.

West passes and partner responds Two Hearts. My particular partner is a reasonable player, not a wild man, so I rebid Three Clubs without too much fear of disaster. Over Three Clubs partner raises to Four Diamonds, invitational I presume. It's possible that partner has a singleton spade, and in any event, I'm not going to linger in a part score when there's a good chance of making a vulnerable game, so I bid Five Diamonds. All pass, so the bidding has been:

NORTH	EAST	SOUTH	WEST
—	—	2♢	Pass
2♡	Pass	3♣	Pass
4♢	Pass	5♢	Pass
Pass	Pass		

West opens the ace of spades. Partner's hand isn't quite what I had expected, but we are still in an excellent contract:

NORTH
♠ 65
♡ Q10975
♢ A107
♣ AK6

SOUTH
♠ 973
♡ —
♢ KQJ986
♣ Q1098

East drops the ten of spades under the ace and West continues with the deuce of spades to East's queen. After winning the second spade, East shifts to a trump which I win in hand. I ruff my last spade in dummy, West playing the eight and East the four.

When I lead a low heart from the dummy, East plays low and I ruff. I lead a diamond to dummy's ace, West pitching the jack of spades, and ruff another heart. I pull the last trump and West lets go of the jack of hearts.

The following cards are left:

NORTH
♠ —
♡ Q10
◇ —
♣ AK6

SOUTH
♠ —
♡ —
◇ J
♣ Q1098

It's time now to gather the evidence and count the hand. East has the missing king of spades, so the spades were divided 4-4. West can't have started with five hearts ace-king-jack, for then he would have entered the bidding; and, he probably would have led a heart rather than the ace of spades.

West must have the ace of hearts, for East had no trouble playing low on the first heart lead from dummy. I can't be positive, but from the play thus far, it appears that West started with four hearts ace-jack. If so, then his distribution must be 4-4-1-4.

Since West has four clubs to East's two, I'm going to run the ten of clubs through him.

The complete hand:

NORTH
- ♠ 65
- ♡ Q10975
- ◇ A107
- ♣ AK6

WEST
- ♠ AJ82
- ♡ AJ84
- ◇ 2
- ♣ 7532

EAST
- ♠ KQ104
- ♡ K632
- ◇ 543
- ♣ J4

SOUTH
- ♠ 973
- ♡ —
- ◇ KQJ986
- ♣ Q1098

I had the distribution pegged properly, but the jack of clubs was with East, not West. East won the club and returned a heart, which I ruffed with my last trump. This left dummy with a losing heart, so I went down two, vulnerable, for minus 200.

It was a sad loss, but at least it brought happiness to two players in the game. West defended the hand well, never pitching a club and I congratulate him for his good defense.

No, I'm not upset at all. Somehow, it amuses me to enter 200 points for my opponents. Partner, on the other hand, doesn't seem amused at all. He sits there with a jaundiced look on his face. He doesn't say a word, but I know he's thinking, "Only a jerk like you could figure a way to go down two on a cold hand."

Hand 22

GOOD PREEMPTS

WHEN PLAYING RUBBER BRIDGE, I tell my partners that I prefer to play very good three bids. I like to play my three bids sound because it makes competition hazardous for the opponents and it averts the large sets that can occur when playing weak preempts. Holding:

♠ AJ109873   ♡ Q54   ◇ A   ♣ 43

I open Three Spades and partner raises me to Four Spades which all pass. The auction has been brief:

NORTH	EAST	SOUTH	WEST
—	—	3♠	Pass
4♠	Pass	Pass	Pass

West leads the jack of hearts and North puts down:

NORTH
♠ Q6
♡ K73
◇ Q10942
♣ A65

SOUTH
♠ AJ109873
♡ Q54
◇ A
♣ 43

We are in a good contract. I can make Four Spades if East holds either the king of spades or the ace of hearts doubleton.

I duck the opening lead in dummy and win the queen of hearts in hand. I'd like to try the spade finesse now, but if I were to lead a club to dummy's ace and the spade finesse lost, then the defense could negotiate a heart ruff if East does in fact hold the ace of hearts doubleton. No, it must be better to duck a club first and finesse the spades later.

West wins the nine of clubs and continues with the ten of hearts. North plays low and East wins with the ace! East returns a diamond which I win with the ace.

I have ten sure tricks now. All I have to do is play the ace of spades and continue with a second trump. No matter how the cards lie, I can hold my losses to one more trick.

But I'm not going to have to give up on the spade finesse yet. It must be safe to enter dummy with the ace of clubs, for if East had seven clubs then he would have given West a club ruff.

When I lead the queen of spades East plays low. I must play safe for ten tricks, so I go up with the ace of spades and surrender a trick to West's doubleton king.

The complete hand:

                        NORTH
                        ♠ Q6
                        ♡ K73
                        ◇ Q10942
                        ♣ A65

WEST   **EAST**
♠ K5   ♠ 42
♡ J10962   ♡ A8
◇ K53   ◇ J876
♣ K109   ♣ QJ872

                        SOUTH
                        ♠ AJ109873
                        ♡ Q54
                        ◇ A
                        ♣ 43

    If declarer immediately enters dummy with the ace of clubs and tries the spade finesse, then West will have an entry in clubs with which to give East a heart ruff and Four Spades may be set. However, by ducking a club first declaror insures the contract whenever East holds the ace of hearts doubleton.

Hand 23

A NEW WHITE SHIRT

WHENEVER I PLAY BRIDGE PROFESSIONALLY, I wear a suit and tie. When someone pays me to play bridge with them, I feel they're entitled to have a presentable partner. Today I put on a new white shirt, one that I've never worn before.

Happily, the A.C.B.L. now separates the smokers from the non-smokers. Since neither partner nor I smoke, we will be playing in one of the non-smoking sections.

Sitting East I hold:

♠ K85   ♡ AK94   ◇ 92   ♣ J653

South, on my left, opens the bidding with One Diamond.

Partner passes, and North responds One Spade. I pass and the opponents reach Five Clubs on this auction:

NORTH	EAST	SOUTH	WEST
—	—	1◇	Pass
1♠	Pass	3♣	Pass
3♠	Pass	4♣	Pass
5♣	Pass	Pass	Pass

Partner leads the jack of hearts and North puts down this dummy:

NORTH
♠ AQJ103
♡ 765
♢ 73
♣ 984

EAST
♠ K85
♡ AK94
♢ 92
♣ J653

I win the king and ace of hearts and South drops the queen. It looks natural now to lead another heart, forcing declarer to ruff. But before playing to the third trick, I reflect on the bidding.

South opened the bidding with One Diamond and thereafter bid and rebid clubs. Hence, South must be either 5-5 or 6-5 in the minors. South's most likely distribution is 1-2-5-5.

If I return a heart now, then declarer will ruff, cash the ace and king of clubs and discover that trumps split 4-1. Declarer will then enter dummy with the ace of spades to finesse against my jack of clubs, making Five Clubs if the diamonds are solid.

That is why I must return a spade, into dummy's ace-queen, before declarer discovers that trumps are split 4-1.

The complete hand:

```
                    NORTH
                    ♠ AQJ103
                    ♡ 765
                    ◇ 73
                    ♣ 984
     WEST                              EAST
     ♠ 9642                           ♠ K85
     ♡ J1082                          ♡ AK94
     ◇ 10654                          ◇ 92
     ♣ 7                              ♣ J653
                    SOUTH
                    ♠ 7
                    ♡ Q3
                    ◇ AKQJ8
                    ♣ AKQ102
```

The spade shift doesn't help declarer. He can pitch one of his diamonds on dummy's ace of spades, but the diamonds were solid anyway. And while declarer still could have made Five Clubs by finessing against my jack of clubs, he didn't know that a first round finesse was necessary. Down one.

□   □   □

After two sessions of bridge, I returned home. When I took off my shirt it was still white and it smelled good.

In past tournaments, before A.C.B.L. separated smokers and non-smokers, my white shirts were always discolored and smelt of tobacco after two sessions of bridge. The introduction of smoking and non-smoking sections is quite an improvement.

Hand 24

THE MARRIED COUPLE

DUPLICATE BRIDGE CLUBS are filled with pugnacious people, especially married couples. From all the shouting and fighting that goes on between them, you'd think that they came to the bridge club for combat rather than to play bridge.

This hand is taken from a local duplicate where my partner and I are playing against a married couple. After arguing for several minutes about the disasters of the previous round, they finally settle down to face current catastrophes.

Both sides are vulnerable and North, on my left, passes. Partner passes, and South opens One Heart. As West I hold:

♠ 10642   ♡ K3   ◇ AQJ1076   ♣ 6

Ordinarily, I'd overcall Two Diamonds. But today I feel like experimenting, so I Double. I have two defensive tricks, and who knows, perhaps partner holds four spades.

The wife, on my left, removes her frown for a moment to bid a loud Two Hearts, no doubt showing good trumps. Partner competes with Three Clubs. South passes and I correct to Three Diamonds. Now North bids a very soft, competitive, Three Hearts which East passes.

Although well aware that his wife's three heart bid was not intended as a game try, South bids Four Hearts anyway, to punish her. Four Hearts is passed around to my partner who Doubles.

The bidding has been:

NORTH	EAST	SOUTH	WEST
Pass	Pass	1♡	Double
2♡	3♣	Pass	3♢
3♡	Pass	4♡	Pass
Pass	Double	Pass	Pass
Pass			

I lead six of clubs. North puts down this dummy:

NORTH
♠ 53
♡ AJ76
♢ 84
♣ Q9842

WEST
♠ 10642
♡ K3
♢ AQJ1076
♣ 6

I'm not pleased to see the ace of hearts in the dummy. We may have a tough time setting Four Hearts.

East wins the ace of clubs and South drops the king. Partner returns the seven of clubs, declarer plays the jack and I ruff. The seven of clubs is a clear suit preference signal for spades. But before mechanically heeding a partner's command to return a spade, I stop to count declarers hand.

Partner cannot have a four card spade suit, for then he would have bid Two Spades over Two Hearts rather than bid Three Clubs. That places South with four spades, five hearts, two clubs, and therefore, two diamonds.

If I return a spade and partner has the ace, then either a club or a diamond return from partner will set four hearts two tricks. But suppose partner holds the king-queen of spades instead of the ace. Then South will win the ace of spades, lead a heart to dummy's ace, picking up my king, pitch one diamond on the queen of clubs, take a ruffing finesse with the club nine and go to dummy with a trump to pitch his last diamond on the established eight of clubs. South will make Four Hearts.

That is why I must cash the ace of diamonds before returning a spade, for the complete hand is:

NORTH
♠ 53
♡ AJ76
◇ 84
♣ Q9842

WEST	EAST
♠ 10642	♠ KQ9
♡ K3	♡ 85
◇ AQJ1076	◇ 532
♣ 6	♣ A10753

SOUTH
♠ AJ87
♡ Q10942
◇ K9
♣ KJ

Cashing the ace of diamonds does not help the declarer. He is able to pitch two of his spades on dummy's clubs but eventually declarer is forced to concede a spade trick, for down one, doubled.

After the hand was over South, knowing that minus 200 would be zero, turned to his wife and told her what a "jackass" she was for bidding Three Hearts. Thereupon she picked up an ashtray and threw it at him.

Producing a blunt instrument from his coat, South assaulted his wife until the director arrived. A delightful couple!

Duplicate bridge can be lots of fun. Real life drama beats the movies any day.

Hand 25

MASTERPOINTS

WHEN YOU ADD UP the cost of transportation, hotel bills and card fees, the average cost of a masterpoint won in a tournament can run as high as $100. No wonder that many players say they wouldn't sell their masterpoints for $10,000.

I, on the other hand, have never placed such high value on the masterpoints which I have won, and in fact, I would be quite happy to sell all of my masterpoints for a very modest amount of money.

Playing in the Open Pairs of a Sectional Tournament with an expert partner against average opponents, I pick up the following hand in the West position:

♠ A72   ♡ K52   ◇ K87   ♣ K1083

The opponents are vulnerable and we are not. South, on my right, is the first to bid and he opens One Spade. I pass and the auction continues:

NORTH	EAST	SOUTH	WEST
—	—	1♠	Pass
2♡	Pass	3♣	Pass
3NT	Pass	4♣	Pass
4♠	Pass	Pass	Pass

I open a low diamond. This looks like a poor choice when this dummy appears:

NORTH
♠ J3
♡ AJ873
◇ QJ109
♣ Q4

WEST
♠ A72
♡ K52
◇ K87
♣ K1083

Fortunately, my opening lead doesn't cost a trick, for South wins the first trick with the ace of diamonds. He leads a spade to dummy's jack, which holds, East dropping the six.

On the second round of trumps, partner plays the five, declarer the king, and I win the ace.

Partner's echo in spades shows that he has another trump, which means declarer started with five spades. Since South bid spades before clubs, I'm inclined to place him with an original distribution of 5-2-1-5.

I shift to the king of hearts which is won by dummy's ace, East playing the six and South the four. Dummy leads the queen of diamonds, declarer pitches a heart, and I win the king. The position now is:

NORTH

♠ —
♡ J873
◇ J10
♣ Q4

WEST

♠ 7
♡ 52
◇ 8
♣ K1083

The obvious play is a heart, forcing declarer to ruff. But a heart won't set Four Spades, for South will ruff, cash a high trump and lead a club toward dummy's queen. Since the trumps are breaking 3-3, declarer will win four trumps, the ace of hearts, three diamonds and two clubs, for a total of ten tricks in all.

I wonder if leading a club would be better. A club lead would take out the entry to the high diamonds. Dummy could cash one diamond, but not both, for I still have a trump left. Yes, a club must be the right play, for then if partner holds either the jack or the nine of clubs, we will set Four Spades.

The complete hand:

NORTH
♠ J3
♡ AJ873
◇ QJ109
♣ Q4

WEST
♠ A72
♡ K52
◇ K87
♣ K1083

EAST
♠ 865
♡ Q106
◇ 65432
♣ 95

SOUTH
♠ KQ1094
♡ 94
◇ A
♣ AJ762

□   □   □

Dummy won the queen of clubs and cashed a high diamond. But no matter how declarer continued, he still had to lose two tricks, for down one.

The rest of our game was not so good. But the afternoon was not spent in vain, for we finished fifth in a fourteen table section, for which we were awarded .60 masterpoints, which was worth $60 at current prices.

Funny, somehow I didn't feel any richer at all.

Hand 26

ENDPLAYED

PLAYING EAST I HOLD:

♠ Q92   ♡ 543   ◇ 763   ♣ Q1096

South, on my left, opens the bidding with One
Diamond. West, my partner, overcalls Two Hearts, weak.
North comes in with a confident Three Clubs and I pass.
The opponents continue to Six Diamonds on this auction.

NORTH	EAST	SOUTH	WEST
—	—	1◇	2♡
3♣	Pass	3NT	Pass
4◇	Pass	4♡	Pass
6◇	Pass	Pass	Pass

Partner leads the king of hearts and North puts down
an impressive dummy:

            NORTH
            ♠ A107
            ♡ 9
            ◇ Q1085
            ♣ AKJ85

                        EAST
                        ♠ Q92
                        ♡ 543
                        ◇ 763
                        ♣ Q1096

South wins the king of hearts with the ace and ruffs a heart in dummy. Next comes a diamond to South's ace, followed by another heart ruff in dummy, and two more rounds of diamonds. Partner shows void on the third round of trumps, pitching a heart, declarer having started with only four diamonds.

This is the position after declarer leads a spade to dummy's ten and my queen:

NORTH
♠ A107
♡ —
◊ —
♣ AKJ8

EAST
♠ Q92
♡ —
◊ —
♣ Q1096

This is embarrassing. I wish I had another heart. I'm endplayed. I don't want to lead a club into dummy's ace-king-jack. Nor do I want to return a spade from the nine. In order to determine the correct return, I attempt to reconstruct South's original distribution.

South started with three hearts and four diamonds. His remaining cards should consist of either four spades and two clubs or three spades and three clubs. Now, if South began with three clubs, then he surely would have saved dummy's fifth club and attempted to establish the clubs. South's original distribution must have been 4-3-4-2, which gives partner an original distribution of 3-6-2-2.

A spade at this point could be disastrous if partner holds the king and South the jack-eight. On the other hand, a club return into dummy's tenace will give declarer only one extra trick in clubs, and will still leave declarer with a losing spade. I am therefore going to return a club into dummy's ace-king-jack.

The complete hand:

NORTH
♠ A107
♡ 9
♢ Q1085
♣ AKJ85

WEST
♠ K53
♡ KQJ1086
♢ 42
♣ 74

EAST
♠ Q92
♡ 543
♢ 763
♣ Q1096

SOUTH
♠ J864
♡ A72
♢ AKJ9
♣ 32

Declarer was able to pitch one of his losing spades on dummy's clubs, but later had to concede a spade trick to partner's king, for down one.

AND THEN THERE WERE FOUR

AFTER CONSIDERABLE RESEARCH, I discovered that there were half a million bridge players in California, three of whom freely admitted they were not experts.

This hand is taken from a rubber bridge game. My left hand opponent is one of those players who claims expert ranking because of his several thousand masterpoints and numerous National victories.

With both sides vulnerable, East, on my right, opens the bidding with One Heart. As South, I hold:

♠ 10963   ♡ 1063   ◇ Q54   ♣ AK7

I pass and West responds One Spade. Partner comes in with Two No-Trump, unusual for the minors, and East passes.

I don't have much defense against the majors, and since my partner is a conservative player who can be counted on to have decent values for his bids, I bid Four Clubs to shut out further competition from West. And who knows, perhaps we have a game.

West, however, thinks we are already too high, for he Doubles.

The bidding has been:

NORTH	EAST	SOUTH	WEST
—	1♡	Pass	1♠
2NT	Pass	4♣	Double
Pass	Pass	Pass	

West leads the ten of diamonds. Partner displays:

NORTH

♠ J
♡ J9
◇ AK963
♣ QJ1094

SOUTH

♠ 10963
♡ 1063
◇ Q54
♣ AK7

It looks as though West has put in a duplicate Double. West is probably 5-3-1-4. With the diamonds divided 4-1, I should be down one in Four Clubs.

I win dummy's king of diamonds and draw three rounds of trump. East follows two rounds and pitches a heart on the third club. East's hand is easy to count. He must be 2-5-4-2. And West must be 6-3-1-3.

There's no hurry to play off the diamonds. I can always concede a diamond later, for down one. Meanwhile, I lead the jack of hearts from dummy. Who knows, perhaps something good will happen.

East covers the jack of hearts with the queen, which holds. Seeing that I am attacking hearts, East plays the ace and queen of spades, which I ruff in dummy. The following cards are left:

                    NORTH
                    ♠ —
                    ♡ 9
                    ◊ A963
                    ♣ 4

WEST   EAST
♠ K875   ♠ —
♡ A7   ♡ K84
◊ —   ◊ J87
♣ —   ♣ —

                    SOUTH
                    ♠ 109
                    ♡ 106
                    ◊ Q5
                    ♣ —

Dummy has only one trump left. It seems prudent now to give up a diamond and settle for down one, for I don't want to go down two. But I'm not willing to settle for down one yet. If I play a second heart and dummy is forced with a third heart, then West will be spade flush and I'll be able to win a trick with the 10-9 of spades. On the other hand, if the opponents force dummy with a spade, then they will be setting up a spade trick for me.

Having decided there is no need to lead a diamond at this point, I continue with another heart. This is passed to West who wins the ace. After some thought West triumphantly returns the king of spades.

He's done it! West has found a way to let me make the hand. I ruff the king of spades in dummy and return to hand with the queen of diamonds. Now the ten of spades squeezes East in hearts and diamonds.

The complete hand:

NORTH
- ♠ J
- ♡ J9
- ◇ AK963
- ♣ QJ1094

WEST
- ♠ K87542
- ♡ A75
- ◇ 10
- ♣ 652

EAST
- ♠ AQ
- ♡ KQ842
- ◇ J872
- ♣ 83

SOUTH
- ♠ 10963
- ♡ 1063
- ◇ Q54
- ♣ AK7

Declarer could hardly have foreseen the squeeze when he led hearts from the dummy. But on many hands the key to success is to punt and hope for the opponents to make a mistake.

□   □   □

While West is trying to find an excuse for leading a spade instead of returning a heart, I make a mental note to reclassify him as a member of the minority faction of non-experts, making four in all.

Hand 28

THE COMEDIAN

♠ AQJ6   ♡ AQ82   ◊ QJ   ♣ Q103

North, on my left, opens the bidding with One No-Trump. Partner passes and South, at my right, bids Four Hearts and it is my bid.

I find myself somewhat unprepared. Holding 18 high card points, I was hoping to bid and make game, perhaps even a slam. Instead, the opponents have bid game against me.

What's more, there's every indication that Four Hearts was bid with the intention of making it, rather than as a preempt.

The question is, should I Double or pass? South ought to have six hearts for his leap to Four Hearts. Partner will likely hold a singleton heart or a void, and consequently, I will probably be limited to two trump tricks on defense. The king of spades is surely at my left, with the opening One No-Trump bidder. Therefore, I will probably win only one spade trick on defense. Neither of my minor suit queens figures to take a trick. In spite of my 18 high card points, we may be unable to set Four Hearts.

Viewed from another perspective, the opponents ought to be able to win the king of spades, four hearts, ace and king of diamonds, and the ace and king of clubs, for a total of nine top tricks. A Double appears somewhat risky, with little to gain, so I pass Four Hearts.

96

The bidding has been:

NORTH	EAST	SOUTH	WEST
1NT	Pass	4♡	Pass
Pass	Pass		

I lead the queen of diamonds. North puts down this dummy :

NORTH
♠ K973
♡ 753
◇ AK82
♣ AJ

WEST
♠ AQJ6
♡ AQ82
◇ QJ
♣ Q103

Declarer wins dummy's ace and king of diamonds, pitching a low spade from hand on the second diamond. Next comes the ace and king of clubs, followed by a club ruff in dummy. Partner follows low on each of the clubs, showing that he originally held five clubs.

Declarer continues with a heart from dummy. Partner shows void, South plays the nine, and I win the queen.

It's time now to reconstruct the hands. Declarer started with six hearts, one diamond, three clubs, and therefore, three spades. Partner began with six diamonds, five clubs, no hearts, and therefore, two spades. This is the position when I win the queen of hearts:

```
                    NORTH
                  ♠ K973
                  ♡ 7
                  ◇ 82
                  ♣ —
WEST
♠ AQJ6                              ♠ ??
♡ A82                              ♡ —
◇ —                                ◇ 10976
♣ —                                ♣ 9
                    SOUTH
                  ♠ ??
                  ♡ KJ1064
                  ◇ —
                  ♣ —
```

I could continue with the ace and queen of spades, but that wouldn't set Four Hearts. Declarer would win dummy's king of spades and continue trump, holding me to only two trump tricks. No, in order to set Four Hearts, I need to put partner on play, so that he can promote a trump trick for me. That is why I must lead the queen of spades at this point, for if partner holds the ten of spades, he can later gain the lead, and Four Hearts will be set.

Declarer wins the king of spades in dummy and continues with another heart to his ten and my ace. At this point I underlead the Ace-Jack of spades. Fortunately, partner wins with the ten of spades. Partner's diamond return promotes my eight of hearts, so we set Four Hearts one trick.

The complete hand:

                      NORTH
                      ♠ K973
                      ♡ 753
                      ◇ AK82
                      ♣ AJ
    WEST   EAST
    ♠ AQJ6   ♠ 104
    ♡ AQ82   ♡ —
    ◇ QJ   ◇ 1097643
    ♣ Q103   ♣ 97652
                      SOUTH
                      ♠ 852
                      ♡ KJ10964
                      ◇ 5
                      ♣ K84

"How'd you like my defense?" I asked partner, quite proud of myself for having underled the Ace-Jack of spades.

"Quite frankly, I think your defense was somewhat anemic," East responds.

"How come?" I inquire, quite surprised at East's evaluation of my play.

"Any red blooded American holding 18 high card points and four trumps should have had enough courage to Double Four Hearts," he responds, "You cost me money."

Hand 29

A DOUBLE-EDGED SWORD

PREEMPTIVE BIDDING often presents the opponents with problems that they find difficult to solve. Of course, it's a double-edged sword, for the partner of the preempting bidder can be misled as well.

Playing rubber bridge with average players I hold:

♠ Q109875   ♡ AJ73   ◇ 87   ♣ 3

Both sides are vulnerable. West, on my left, opens the bidding with Three Clubs. Partner Doubles and East jumps to Five Clubs. I don't suppose that they can make Five Clubs, but I'm not about to defend with ten cards in the majors, so I bid Five Spades.

West Doubles. Have I done the wrong thing? We shall see. Partner and East consider their holdings for a while, but eventually all pass.

The bidding has been:

NORTH	EAST	SOUTH	WEST
—	—	—	3♣
Double	5♣	5♠	Double
Pass	Pass	Pass	

The opening lead is the five of hearts. Apologizing for having only two trumps, partner puts down:

NORTH
♠ AJ
♡ KQ984
◇ AK632
♣ A

SOUTH
♠ Q109875
♡ AJ73
◇ 87
♣ 4

Partner needn't apologize with such a powerful hand. Our opponent's preemptive tactics have kept us out of a lay down slam. Six Hearts is cold. Even Six Spades ought to be a make.

I win the opening heart lead in hand and lead a spade to dummy's ace. All follow. Five spades is cold now. All I have to do now is overtake dummy's jack of spades.

First, however, I am going to give some thought to West's distribution. I'm sure he has a singleton heart and seven clubs. And he probably holds three or four spades to the king for his double.

A vulnerable overtrick doubled is worth 200 points. There'll be no trouble in making an overtrick if West's distribution is 3-1-2-7. But if West is 4-1-1-7, then he will win the king of spades and put me back on board with a club or a diamond and I won't be able to prevent him from making a small trump by ruffing a diamond or a heart.

That is why I must cash dummy's ace of clubs and ace of diamonds before leading a second trump. East, as expected, shows out and I overtake dummy's jack of spades with the queen. West wins the king of spades, but he is now unable to prevent me from picking up the rest of his trumps, so I make an overtrick, doubled.

The complete hand:

```
                    NORTH
                    ♠ AJ
                    ♡ KQ984
                    ◇ AK632
                    ♣ A
    WEST                              EAST
    ♠ K643                           ♠ 2
    ♡ 5                              ♡ 1062
    ◇ 4                              ◇ QJ1095
    ♣ KQJ10875                       ♣ 9632
                    SOUTH
                    ♠ Q109875
                    ♡ AJ73
                    ◇ 87
                    ♣ 4
```

"I'm sorry I Doubled, partner," said West, "but I thought it was our hand."

"I knew they'd make Five Spades," said East, "but I was afraid to bid Six Clubs vulnerable."

In fact, Six Clubs Doubled would have gone down only three tricks, with a hundred honors, for minus 800, a considerable savings over the 1050 points actually lost.

THE IMPATIENT MAN

MY RIGHT HAND OPPONENT IS AN IMPATIENT MAN at the bridge table. He's always trying to speed up the game. It seems he can't even tolerate a few moments delay in the play of the cards.

With both sides vulnerable, I hold as South:

♠ 82   ♡ KJ62   ◇ AKJ107   ♣ 72

I open the bidding with One Diamond. West, on my left, overcalls Two Spades, weak. Partner bids a cheerful Three Clubs and East moans a pass. I rebid Three diamonds, West passes and partner, one of the world's great cardholders, raises me to Six Diamonds, which all pass.

The bidding has been:

NORTH	EAST	SOUTH	WEST
—	—	1◇	2♠
3♣	Pass	3◇	Pass
6◇	Pass	Pass	Pass

West leads the king of spades. North, full of pride, puts down this powerful dummy:

NORTH
♠ A4
♡ A3
◇ Q54
♣ AK9843

SOUTH
♠ 82
♡ KJ62
◇ AKJ107
♣ 72

Wrong contract! We belong in Seven Diamonds, which requires only a 3-2 club split. But the clubs may be breaking 4-1, in which case even Six Diamonds may not make. I must plan the play to handle a possible 4-1 club split.

A review of the available entries shows that I cannot ruff two hearts in dummy. I can ruff one heart, but that won't help me. Further, by ruffing a heart in dummy, I remove the entry to the clubs.

I see two possible lines of play. The first is to duck the opening lead, pull the trumps and ruff a club. If the clubs don't split, then I can run the trumps, play the ace of hearts and finesse the jack of hearts, squeezing East if he holds four hearts and four clubs.

The second line of play is to pull two rounds of trumps and then play the ace and king of clubs and ruff a club, followed by a trump to dummy's queen and another club ruff. This line of play works only when the hand with the singleton club holds precisely two diamonds.

Which is the better line? I can't decide, but I'm inclined to go with the second line of play, for the first line of play requires a finesse as well as a certain distribution. For the moment, however, I'm going to delay making a decision on which line of play to adopt.

My analysis of the play thus far has taken less than a minute. East, however, shows his impatience.

"Hurry up and play," he growls, "You can't possibly have any problem making Six Diamonds with that dummy." I trust his analysis will prove correct.

It can't hurt to duck the king of spades. And who knows? Perhaps I'll be lucky and receive a heart shift from West. West however, continues with a second spade to dummy's ace.

I play the ace and jack of trumps and all follow. On the second round of trumps, East drops the nine. That's interesting! East's impatience has shown he's not putting much effort into the defense. Hence, East is not falsecarding.

If anyone holds a singleton club, it will be West. And since West holds the missing eight of diamonds, the second line of play will not succeed. If the clubs break 4-1, I'll have to rely upon the heart finesse and a squeeze to make Six Diamonds.

I pull the last trump and West, as expected, follows, East pitching a low spade. When I play the ace and king of clubs, they prove to be 4-1, West holding a singleton.

I ruff a club to hand and play my last trump. East is forced to pitch a heart from four in order to protect the clubs. Now a heart to the ace, followed by the finesse of the jack of hearts yields four heart tricks, so I make Six Diamonds.

The complete hand:

NORTH
- ♠ A4
- ♡ A3
- ◇ Q54
- ♣ AK9843

WEST
- ♠ KQJ1065
- ♡ 975
- ◇ 863
- ♣ Q

EAST
- ♠ 973
- ♡ Q1084
- ◇ 92
- ♣ J1065

SOUTH
- ♠ 82
- ♡ KJ62
- ◇ AKJ107
- ♣ 72

East is upset that Six Diamonds was made against him on a finesse and a squeeze. He interrupts a discussion between partner and me regarding the play of the hand.

"Let's get on with the game," says East, "There's no reason for it to be this slow."

At East's request, we gather in the cards and begin dealing the next hand. Of course, I never tell East that I relied upon the fall of his nine of diamonds as natural to make the hand.

Hand 31

THE AVERAGE PLAYER

THERE ARE MANY HANDS in which I can present a problem to an opponent, knowing he will make a predictable response. This is one of those hands.

Playing in a rubber bridge game against opponents of average ability, I pick up:

♠ A9653   ♡ 2   ◇ A73   ♣ KJ76

Neither side is vulnerable and I am first to bid. I open One Spade. West passes and partner responds Three Spades.

At partner's insistence, we are not playing limit raises, so I take his bid as forcing. I have nothing extra, so I bid Four Spades, which all pass.

The bidding has been:

NORTH	EAST	SOUTH	WEST
—	—	1♠	Pass
3♠	Pass	4♠	Pass
Pass	Pass		

West leads the queen of hearts and partner puts down this dummy:

NORTH

♠ Q1087
♡ K654
◇ KQ
♣ Q52

SOUTH

♠ A9653
♡ 2
◇ A73
♣ KJ76

I duck the queen of hearts. West shifts to the three of clubs and I play low in dummy. East wins the ace of clubs and returns the nine of clubs which I win in dummy with the queen, West playing the four.

The obvious play now is the ace and another spade, which loses two trump tricks only when East holds the king-jack third or fourth. It's silly to consider running the queen of spades through East, for it's likely that West holds four clubs and he may be able to give East a club ruff.

Before playing the ace of spades, however, I lead a low heart from the table. East plays the ace and I ruff. That's different! East isn't the sort of player who would play the ace of hearts without a doubleton.

East's play of the ace of hearts marks West with six hearts. And West's play of the clubs has shown that he holds at least three and probably four clubs. Now, if West had a singleton diamond, then he probably would have led it earlier in hopes of obtaining a ruff. Since West didn't lead a diamond, I'm going to assume that he holds at least two diamonds, and therefore, West holds at most two spades.

I enter dummy with the queen of diamonds and lead the queen of spades. All I have to do now is guess the trump position, for West can't have the king-jack third. If East plays low on the queen of spades, I shall play the ace, expecting West to hold either a singleton honor or the doubleton king. But East obligingly covers the queen of spades with the king. I win with the ace and return a spade, making Four Spades.

Thre complete hand:

NORTH
♠ Q1087
♡ K654
◇ KQ
♣ Q52

WEST
♠ 4
♡ QJ10983
◇ 84
♣ 10843

EAST
♠ KJ2
♡ A7
◇ J109652
♣ A9

SOUTH
♠ A9653
♡ 2
◇ A73
♣ KJ76

It was nice of East to cover the queen of spades. Of course, I don't tell him that I would have played the ace of spades on the queen if he had played low. East's only chance to set Four Spades was to duck the queen of trumps when it was led but, like most players, he wasn't prepared for the play.

Hand 32

LEISURE TIME ACTIVITIES

MY PARTNER IS A BEAUTIFUL YOUNG WOMAN who devotes all of her time leisure time to playing duplicate bridge. She's delighted to play bridge with me and she plays bridge with me whenever she can.

As for me, even though she's not a great player, I truly enjoy her company. She's a princess. And while we are not contemplating marriage, we are sharing a room together.

Sitting East I hold:

♠ 632   ♡ 94   ◇ J9864   ♣ J96

South, on my left, opens the bidding with One Spade. Partner overcalls Two Hearts and North makes a limit raise of Three Spades. I pass and South, after a slight pause, bids Four Spades, which all pass.

The bidding has been:

NORTH	EAST	SOUTH	WEST
—	—	1♠	2♡
3♠	Pass	4♠	Pass
Pass	Pass		

Partner leads the king of hearts and North puts down this dummy:

NORTH
- ♠ AJ97
- ♡ 8653
- ◇ A5
- ♣ 854

EAST
- ♠ 632
- ♡ 94
- ◇ J9864
- ♣ J96

Partner cashes the king and ace of hearts and declarer drops the queen. Partner continues with the jack of hearts, I discard a low diamond, and South ruffs.

Declarer plays the ace and king of spades and partner pitches one of her remaining hearts. South continues with the ace and king of diamonds and a diamond ruff in dummy. West shows with the queen third of diamonds.

North leads the fourth round of hearts in this position:

NORTH
- ♠ J
- ♡ 8
- ◇ —
- ♣ 854

EAST
- ♠ 6
- ♡ —
- ◇ J
- ♣ J96

South's hand is easy to count. He started with five spades, two hearts, three diamonds, and therefore, three clubs.

To set Four Spades, the defense will have to win two tricks in clubs. Therefore, I need partner to hold at least the king-ten of clubs.

Now, if I were to pitch on dummy's last heart, then declarer also might pitch on the heart, and partner would be endplayed, forced to lead a club to declarer's possible ace-queen. That is why I must ruff the heart.

Declarer overruffs the heart and leads his last trump to dummy's jack of spades. I let go of the jack of diamonds. At this point, the only cards left in play are clubs.

This is the position when dummy leads a low club:

NORTH
♠ —
♡ —
◇ —
♣ 854

EAST
♠ —
♡ —
◇ —
♣ J96

I can't afford to let declarer duck the club to partner, so I go with the nine of clubs. Declarer finesses the queen and partner wins the king. Fortunately, partner holds the ten of clubs, so we set Four Spades one trick.

This was the complete hand:

NORTH
♠ AJ97
♡ 8653
◇ A5
♣ 854

WEST
♠ 4
♡ AKJ102
◇ Q103
♣ K1032

EAST
♠ 632
♡ 94
◇ J9864
♣ J96

SOUTH
♠ KQ1085
♡ Q7
◇ K72
♣ AQ7

The hand was interesting in that East, with two bare jacks, must defend well or declarer will make Four Spades.

☐   ☐   ☐

Following the end of the evening session, partner waits to ascertain our standing and is pleased to learn that we have placed third overall.

"I have a suggestion," I say. "Why don't we take tommorrow off and go to the beach or a movie? After all we've played bridge four days in a row now."

"I don't want to," she replies, "This is my vacation and I want to play bridge every day."

I concede. Bridge was her favorite leisure time activity. And it wasn't a burden for me to play bridge with her for nine days in a row. I had done it before.

Hand 33

THE VENDOR

I HAD A LOT OF ERRANDS TO RUN THIS MORNING. As a result, I skipped breakfast, arriving at a local Sectional Tournament just in time to make the afternoon session. As soon as the first round is over, I'm going to get something to eat.

Playing South I hold:

♠ KQ8754   ♡ KQ3   ◊ 42   ♣ 75

East, at my right, opens the bidding with One Club. Partner and I play our jump overcalls like a sound weak two bid, so I bid Two Spades. West passes and North raises me to Four Spades, which all pass.

The bidding has been:

NORTH	EAST	SOUTH	WEST
—	1♣	2♠	Pass
4♠	Pass	Pass	Pass

West leads the deuce of clubs. North puts down this dummy:

NORTH
♠ J10
♡ AJ74
♢ AK73
♣ 963

SOUTH
♠ KQ8754
♡ KQ3
♢ 42
♣ 75

East wins the king and queen of clubs and continues with the ace. I ruff the third round of clubs low, West showing with three clubs to the jack. I lead a spade to dummy's jack and ten, both of which hold. On the second spade West shows void, pitching a low heart, East having started with four spades A-9-x-x.

The hand looks simple enough. I have ten top tricks. All I have to do is return to hand with the king of hearts and lead the king and queen of spades, picking up East's nine.

I foresee a possible snag, however. East appears to have started with four spades and five clubs. Most likely, his original distribution was 4-1-3-5 or 4-3-1-5. Now if I were to return to hand with a heart, East could win the ace of spades and put me on the board with a diamond. Then I'd have to guess how to exit safely from dummy.

That is why I must cash the ace of diamonds before leading a heart from dummy. East follows to both the ace of diamonds and the heart. When I lead the king of spades, East wins the ace. But no matter how he continues, I have the rest of the tricks.

115

The complete hand:

NORTH
♠ J10
♡ AJ74
◇ AK73
♣ 963

WEST
♠ 2
♡ 982
◇ J109865
♣ J82

EAST
♠ A963
♡ 1065
◇ Q
♣ AKQ104

SOUTH
♠ KQ8754
♡ KQ3
◇ 42
♣ 75

West defended the hand well by pitching a low heart on the second round of spades rather than one of his six diamonds. The heart discard makes it difficult for declarer to guess the distribution correctly.

Without the play of the ace of diamonds at trick four, I could have easily gone down in Four Spades. When East later wins the ace of spades and returns the queen of diamonds, declarer is put to a difficult guess how to exit from dummy.

As it turns out, East could have set Four Spades by returning the queen of diamonds at trick two and later underleading his ace-king of clubs for a diamond ruff, but this was a difficult defense.

□   □   □

After the first round ended, I went to the refreshment stand and ordered a cup of coffee and a tuna sandwich.

"That'll be ten dollars," said the man in charge of the refreshment counter.

116

"Ten dollars!" I exclaimed with surprise at the amount demanded. The same order from a cafeteria would have cost less than half as much.

"That's right," said the vendor. "The coffee is two dollars and the sandwich is eight dollars."

Hand 34

THE MASTER DEFENDER

MOST HOME TEAM OF FOUR GAMES in which I play consist of random pairs. But tonight things are different, for all the players are experts.

With IMP scoring being used, I hold as South:

♠ K109865   ♡ A6542   ◊ 3   ♣ Q

Both sides are vulnerable. Left hand opponent opens a strong One No-Trump, which is passed to me.

Fortunately, partner and I are playing Brozel, a convention in which overcalls over One No-Trump show specific two-suiters. With a normal one suited overcall we Double, forcing partner to respond Two Clubs, after which we pass or bid our suit.

I bid Two Hearts, which shows hearts and spades. West passes and partner passes. East gives this some consideration, but also passes.

The bidding has been:

NORTH	EAST	SOUTH	WEST
—	—	—	1NT
Pass	Pass	2♡	Pass
Pass	Pass		

West leads the ten of hearts. Partner puts down:

NORTH
♠ Q
♡ QJ3
◇ J872
♣ K9762

SOUTH
♠ K109865
♡ A6542
◇ 3
♣ Q

Not bad at all. If hearts and spades behave normally, Two Hearts should be cold.

I cover the ten of hearts with dummy's jack, East plays the king and I win the ace. I'm just about to lead a spade to dummy's queen when I foresee a possible snag.

My left hand opponent is a master defender. I know him well. He's mean and nasty, just the sort of person who would let me hold the queen of spades. That would leave me an entry short of setting up the suit.

Yes indeed! Against a player of his caliber, I shall have to take the precaution of starting the spades by leading the king. But first, I must lead a heart to dummy's jack, for this is my last chance to extract a second round of trumps and I don't want East to make a low trump ruffing spades.

Both opponents follow to the second trump. I continue by leading dummy's queen of spades and overtaking with my king. After this play the hand is quite simple. The defense wins two spades, a trump, and a trick in each minor, so I make exactly Two Hearts.

The complete hand:

```
                    NORTH
                    ♠ Q
                    ♡ QJ3
                    ◊ J872
                    ♣ K9762
   WEST                            EAST
   ♠ AJ3                           ♠ 742
   ♡ 1098                          ♡ K7
   ◊ AK94                          ◊ Q1065
   ♣ A105                          ♣ J843
                    SOUTH
                    ♠ K109865
                    ♡ A6542
                    ◊ 3
                    ♣ Q
```

Bridge is a game of psychology. It's frequently good strategy to play the same hand in a different manner against opponents of disproportionate skill. Against average opponents declarer should start the spades by leading low toward dummy's queen. He need fear a duck only from an expert defender.

If West ducks the queen of spades then South will be unable to set up and cash the spades. Thereafter, good defense would limit declarer to seven tricks.

At the second table the contract was Two Spades, which had no chance after repeated diamond leads by the defense. Two Spades was set one trick, for a net swing of 210 points, or 5 imps.

Chapter 35

THE GAMBLER

THIS HAND COMES FROM NEW YORK CITY where the rubber bridge clubs stay open twenty-four hours. Being restless, I go to my regular bridge club. The South player in my game is a typical gambler. She's a housewife who regularly converts her rent money into bridge losses. I hate to play against players who can't afford to lose, but it's 3 a.m. on a Thursday morning and there's no other game.

We are vulnerable and they are not. I hold:

♠ AJ7   ♡ 854   ◊ J9873   ♣ 103

South, on my left, opens One Spade. Partner passes and North responds Two Clubs. I pass and the auction continues:

NORTH	EAST	SOUTH	WEST
—	—	1 ♠	Pass
2 ♣	Pass	2 ♡	Pass
3 ♠	Pass	4 ♠	Pass
Pass	Pass		

Partner leads the king of diamonds. North puts down this dummy:

NORTH
♠ KQ8
♡ 1062
◊ A52
♣ KQ65

EAST
♠ AJ7
♡ 854
◊ J9873
♣ 103

Even though I have two trump tricks the defensive outlook is bleak, for partner can't hold more than the king or queen of hearts in addition to the king-queen of diamonds.

Declarer wins the ace of diamonds in dummy. Anxious to pitch her losing diamond, declarer leads a club to her ace and a club to dummy's king. Declarer then leads the queen of clubs from dummy and it's my play.

There's no use in discarding a heart on the third round of clubs, for then South will discard her losing diamond and the defense will come to only two trump tricks and a heart.

Likewise, if I ruff with the jack of spades, declarer will still shed her losing diamond, losing only another trump and a heart.

Can there be any merit in ruffing with the seven of spades?

Possibly. If South overruffs, then I can win the first trump and put partner in with a diamond and make the jack of spades by ruffing a club. Even if South pitches her losing diamond when I ruff, she'll still have to guess the location of the jack of spades to make the hand. And it can't cost to ruff low, for whatever South does to the defense must still come to at least two tricks in diamonds and spades.

I ruff when the seven of spades and declarer pitches her losing diamond. Now the play must be to put partner on lead so that I can ruff another club with the jack of spades. Therefore, I shift to a low heart. South rises with the ace and leads a low spade to dummy's king and my ace.

On the lead of a second heart South is faced with a difficult guess. She finesses the heart, playing me for the queen of hearts or West for the jack of spades. But partner wins the queen of hearts and plays a club, which allows me to make the jack of spades.

The complete hand:

```
                    NORTH
                  ♠ KQ8
                  ♡ 1062
                  ◇ A52
                  ♣ KQ65
     WEST                          EAST
   ♠ 42                          ♠ AJ7
   ♡ Q93                         ♡ 854
   ◇ KQ10                        ◇ J9873
   ♣ J9842                       ♣ 103
                    SOUTH
                  ♠ 109653
                  ♡ AKJ7
                  ◇ 64
                  ♣ A7
```

The pause to consider what trump to play on dummy's queen of clubs was conveniently arranged for this narrative. In practice, the problem was solved earlier. To have hesitated before ruffing the club would have given the show away, for there would have been no problem at all with just the A-7 of trumps.

□   □   □

I returned to the bridge club on Sunday afternoon. Once again I was invited to play in the game with the gambling housewife. This time there were other games available, so I declined.

An inquiry which I directed to the owner of the bridge club brought an expected reply: she hadn't gone home since Thursday!

Bridge is a great pastime for most players. Unfortunately, like most activities, it can be abused until it becomes a means of self-destruction. Rubber bridge especially can be a problem the gambler, for the gambler gambles to lose.

THE OBNOXIOUS MAN

MY RIGHT HAND OPPONENT has just called the director to the table on a trivial matter. My partner failed to alert him that my Two Diamond response was artificial in an action that began:

NORTH	EAST	SOUTH	WEST
2♣	Pass	2 ◊	

How could anyone be so petty? It's ridiculous, especially in the Mixed Pairs of a National Tournament where all of the participants are experienced players. Some people, however, enjoy being rude.

On the second board, I hold as South:

♠ AKQJ42   ♡ 52   ◊ K   ♣ AK96

Neither side is vulnerable. West, on my left opens the bidding with Four Hearts. This is passed to me and I bid Four Spades. We may miss a slam if parner has a good hand, but I have no other call. Everyone passes, so the bidding has been:

NORTH	EAST	SOUTH	WEST
—	—	—	4 ♡
Pass	Pass	4 ♠	Pass
Pass	Pass		

West leads the king of hearts and North puts down:

NORTH
♠ 75
♡ 973
◇ AJ64
♣ 7542

SOUTH
♠ AKQJ42
♡ 52
◇ K
♣ AK96

West cashes the first two hearts and continues with a third heart. East follows to the second round of hearts. On the third heart, East drops the seven of diamonds. I ruff with the four of spades, preserving the deuce, and cash two rounds of trump. West shows out on the second round of spades.

This is the type of hand where it's easy to relax, only to go down one. Ten tricks are easily made with a normal split in clubs. The question is, can I make Four Spades against a 4-1 club split?

If East holds the four clubs, then I can can make Four Spades only when East also holds the queen of diamonds, for then I can squeeze him on the run of the spades. Somehow that seems unlikely, for East pitched a high diamond on the third heart. I don't think that East would have pitched a diamond so easily with Q-x-x if his distribution were 4-2-3-4.

Suppose that West holds the four clubs. West's distribution would then be 1-6-2-4, which would give East a distribution of 4-2-6-1. If so, I could endplay East to lead into dummy's diamonds. Yes, indeed! In fact, I hope that the clubs don't split, for I am going to enjoy the hand if that's the case.

I continue by drawing one more round of trump, which leaves East with one remaining spade. Next, I cash the king of diamonds and continue with the ace and king of clubs. If the clubs split, I'll pull East's last trump and concede a club, making Four Spades.

But the clubs are divided 4-1, as I had hoped. After studying the king of clubs for a while, East pitches a diamond. Well, it won't help him. I lead the deuce of spades to his ten, putting East on play with nothing but diamonds to lead into dummy's ace-jack. This allows me to discard both of my losing clubs, so I make Four Spades.

The complete hand:

```
                    NORTH
                    ♠ 75
                    ♡ 973
                    ◇ AJ64
                    ♣ 7542
        WEST                        EAST
        ♠ 6                         ♠ 10983
        ♡ AKQJ104                   ♡ 86
        ◇ 85                        ◇ Q109732
        ♣ QJ108                     ♣ 3
                    SOUTH
                    ♠ AKQJ42
                    ♡ 52
                    ◇ K
                    ♣ AK96
```

After the hand is scored, it occurs to me that it was necessary to ruff the third round of hearts with the four of spades. I take East's hand out of the duplicate board. Sure enough, East's spades were the 10-9-8-3. If I had ruffed with the deuce, East could have set me by unblocking the spades.

□   □   □

"DIRECTOR!" cries East in a nasty tone. What's going on? Why is East so angry? Presently, the director arrives.

"THAT MAN," says East, pointing at me, "took my hand out of the duplicate board without asking permission."

The director advises me that I have violated the rules. I should have summoned him to the table to supervise while I examined East's hand.

"You're right again and I do apologize," I say to East. But all the while I am thinking to myself what an unpleasant fellow he really is. Anyone else would have had enough charity to overlook this minor offense.

HALF A MATCH POINT

PLAYING DUPLICATE BRIDGE with an expert partner, I hold as East:

♠ A73   ♡ 1093   ◇ A6   ♣ Q10972

Neither side is vulnerable. South, on my left, opens the bidding with One Spade. West passes and North responds Two Clubs. I pass and our opponents bid game in spades on this auction:

NORTH	EAST	SOUTH	WEST
—	—	1♠	Pass
2♣	Pass	2♡	Pass
3NT	Pass	4♠	Pass
Pass	Pass		

Lately, my partner and I have been playing a lead convention which we find works rather well. We lead low from an odd number of cards in a suit and third best from an even number of cards in a suit.

Partner leads a deuce of diamonds, showing three or five, and North puts down this dummy:

NORTH
♠ 106
♡ 654
◇ KQJ10
♣ AK43

EAST
♠ A73
♡ 1093
◇ A6
♣ Q10972

From the auction, South should hold six spades and four hearts. Partner's opening lead marks declarer with two diamonds, so South's distribution ought to be 6-4-2-1.

I win the opening lead with the ace of diamonds. It looks normal to shift to a heart. But I don't think a heart shift is necessary now, for I can kill the dummy by returning a club. Then any heart tricks we have coming will later accrue to us.

I return the queen of clubs at the second trick. South drops the jack, partner follows with the five, and dummy's king wins the trick. Declarer leads the six of spades to his king and continues with another trump which I win with the ace.

Now I return a diamond. This cuts declarer off from the dummy. Declarer is able to cash a club for a heart discard, but when he tries to cash a diamond I ruff. South overruffs, but eventually he is forced to surrender a trick to partner's queen of hearts.

The complete hand:

$$
\begin{array}{c}
\textbf{NORTH} \\
\spadesuit\ 106 \\
\heartsuit\ 654 \\
\diamondsuit\ KQJ10 \\
\clubsuit\ AK43
\end{array}
$$

WEST
♠ 42
♡ Q87
◇ 98752
♣ 865

EAST
♠ A73
♡ 1093
◇ A6
♣ Q10972

SOUTH
♠ KQJ985
♡ AKJ2
◇ 43
♣ J

Note how accurate our lead convention was on this hand. The lead of a low diamond immediately marked South with a doubleton. Without an exact count, East is ill placed to defend properly.

□   □   □

Our defense proved to be needlessly acute. Most of the other North-South pairs played in Three No-trump by North. After the lead of a low club to dummy's jack, they had no difficulty in making Five No-Trump. But holding declarer to Four Spades did make a difference of half a match point.

Hand 38

A CRITICAL PARTNER

WHENEVER I PLAY RUBBER BRIDGE, I try not to criticize my partners. It never does any good. Finding fault tends to upset your partners and it puts them in a poor frame of mind to play well on the following hands.

Playing rubber bridge with a partner who was critical of my defense on the previous hand, I hold:

♠ AQ109652   ♡ J3   ◊ 654   ♣ 2

We are vulnerable and they are not. Partner opens One Club. While I am wondering whether to respond One Spade or Three Spades, East, on my right, bids Four Hearts.

This is a difficult hand to evaluate. If partner holds secondary values in clubs or any honors in hearts, then we probably should defend. On the other hand, if partner holds the king of spades and some strength in diamonds, then we ought to be able to make Four Spades.

I've played the game before. I'm not going to let East push me around. I bid Four Spades. When West Doubles, I know I've made a poor decision.

The bidding, not very elegant on my part, has been:

NORTH	EAST	SOUTH	WEST
1♣	4♡	4♠	Double
Pass	Pass	Pass	

132

West leads the four of hearts. Partner puts down a standard dummy for me:

NORTH
♠ 87
♡ K6
◇ A72
♣ KQJ976

SOUTH
♠ AQ109652
♡ J3
◇ 654
♣ 2

Wonderful! It looks like we're going down four doubled, vulnerable, against a non-makable Four Hearts. Why did I bid Four Spades?

East cashes the first two heart tricks, West echoing with the deuce, to show a doubleton. East then shifts to the queen of diamonds, I play low from hand, West plays the ten of diamonds, and I duck in dummy. East continues with the jack of diamonds, which I win in dummy with the ace.

Is there any chance of saving a trick? Each undertrick costs 300 points. Let's see. If East holds the ace of clubs and no more diamonds, then I might be able to pitch my remaining diamond on dummy's clubs. But first, I must remove his card of exit.

I lead a spade to my ace, East playing the four and West the three. Now I lead a club to dummy's king. East wins the ace, but he has no more diamonds to play. Having nothing but clubs and hearts left, East elects to return a heart, which allows me to pitch my losing diamond, so I am down only three, doubled, vulnerable, for minus 800, a wonderful result!

The complete hand:

NORTH
♠ 87
♡ K6
◇ A72
♣ KQJ976

WEST
♠ KJ3
♡ 42
◇ K10983
♣ 854

EAST
♠ 4
♡ AQ109875
◇ QJ
♣ A103

SOUTH
♠ AQ109652
♡ J3
◇ 654
♣ 2

This hand was not difficult to play. I included it with a point in mind. Too often, when players wind up in a disastrous contract, they get upset and fail to play their best game. They relax and fail to fight for the best possible result. And the results they achieve are much worse than they ought to be. But at 300 points an undertrick, it pays to put in the maximum effort to limit your losses.

□　　　□　　　□

"Couldn't we have set them two in Four Hearts?", asked my partner at the end of the hand. "Wouldn't that have been a better result than going for 800?"

"Yes," I replied, "We could have set them two in Four Hearts. Thanks for pointing it out to me. I hadn't noticed." Next time I play with him, I'll go for 1100.

"Let's get on with the next hand," I said, realizing that North had got me into the perfect mood to be his partner on the next deal.

Hand 39

TWO FAST PASSES

BRIDGE PLAYERS vary their manner of bidding because it's human to do so. Most do so innocently, not by design. But too often they transmit information about their hands which could influence their partner's actions.

Of course, these nuances in the bidding are observable by their opponents as well as their partners. On this hand, two fast passes help the declarer make his contract.

Playing in the Open Pairs of a Regional Tournament with an expert partner against strangers, I hold as South:

♠ 42   ♡ AQJ8   ◊ AQ1086   ♣ 83

East is first to bid and he opens the bidding with One Club. I overcall One Heart, rather than One Diamond, as I don't want to lose the heart suit in event that West bids spades.

West, however, passes quickly, leaving no doubt that he's not at all well fixed in high cards. Partner bids Three Clubs, a conventional call in our system, which shows a maximum limit raise with four trumps. East seems surprised at partner's call, but he doesn't bother to ask the meaning of that bid. Knowing that it's not his hand, East also passes quickly. Since I hold a good hand, with above average values for an overcall, I bid Four Hearts, which all pass.

The bidding has been:

NORTH	EAST	SOUTH	WEST
—	1♣	1♡	Pass
3♣	Pass	4♡	Pass
Pass	Pass		

West opens with an ace of clubs. The dummy is just about what I had expected:

NORTH
♠ 8765
♡ K965
◇ K43
♣ KQ

SOUTH
♠ 42
♡ AQJ8
◇ AQ1086
♣ 83

East drops the jack of clubs under the ace, some kind of suit preference signal I imagine. West dutifully switches to the jack of spades which East overtakes with the queen. East cashes the ace of spades and West drops the three. East continues with the ace of spades and it's my play.

Could East have a five card spade suit? I doubt it. With five spades A-K-Q-10-x, East probably would have opened the bidding with One Spade. If not, East certainly would have given some thought to bidding Three Spades over partner's Three Club bid. But East passed Three Clubs quickly, which confirms that he does not hold five spades. Having settled the spade position, I ruff the third round of spades low, with the eight of hearts. West as expected follows with a third spade.

136

I cash the ace and queen of hearts. East shows out on the second round, pitching a club. The following cards are left:

NORTH
♠ 8
♡ K9
◊ K43
♣ K

SOUTH
♠ —
♡ J
◊ AQ1086
♣ 8

The hand looks easy now. All I have to do is pick up the trumps and run the diamonds. Then only four diamonds to the jack in the West hand would set me, a possibility that seems quite remote, for that would give East a distribution of 4-1-1-7.

Still, I'd like to test the diamonds before drawing trump. But then if East started with four diamonds, West would ruff the second round. Wait a minute! If West has a singleton diamond, then his hand would be:

♠ J10x   ♡ 10xxx   ◊ x   ♣ Axxxx

Surely, with five clubs to the ace and a singleton, West would have bid Two Clubs over my One Heart overcall. West would have at least considered bidding Two Clubs. But West passed quickly, which shows that he can't possibly hold a singleton diamond and five clubs to the ace.

I cash the ace of diamonds and lead a diamond to dummy's king. On the second diamond East shows void, pitching a club. So East was 4-1-1-7 after all!

The rest of the play is easy. I play dummy's high club and my queen of diamonds and cross-ruff the remainder of the tricks, making Four Hearts.

The complete hand:

                    NORTH
                    ♠ 8765
                    ♡ K965
                    ◇ K43
                    ♣ KQ
    WEST   **EAST**
    ♠ J103   ♠ AKQ9
    ♡ 10742   ♡ 5
    ◇ J975   ◇ 2
    ♣ A7   ♣ J1096542
                    SOUTH
                    ♠ 42
                    ♡ AQJ8
                    ◇ AQ1086
                    ♣ 83

Without West's fast passes declarer could easily have gone wrong on this hand. To make Four Hearts declarer must guess to ruff the third spade low and he must test the diamonds before drawing a third round of trumps.

Hand 40

OFFER REJECTED

WHEN PLAYING RUBBER BRIDGE, I have the habit of estimating my potential gain or loss on each hand before the bidding is completed. And I frequently make a silent offer of compromise, as though I could settle for a specific gain or loss.

Playing in my regular rubber bridge game, I pick up one of my usual hands as East:

♠ Q8   ♡ 732   ◇ 54   ♣ Q109542

Both sides are vulnerable and West, my partner, passes. Wonderful! I hope my opponents don't bid a slam. I'd gladly settle to give them a game.

But my silent offer is rejected, for the opponents bid to Six Hearts on this auction:

NORTH	EAST	SOUTH	WEST
—	—	—	Pass
1◇	Pass	1♡	Pass
2♡	Pass	4NT	Pass
5♡	Pass	6♡	Pass
Pass	Pass		

Partner opens the three of clubs and North puts down:

NORTH
♠ J73
♡ AQ6
◇ AKQ62
♣ 86

EAST
♠ Q8
♡ 732
◇ 54
♣ Q109542

Declarer wins the queen of clubs with the ace. After some thought, declarer cashes the jack of hearts, the ace of hearts, and the king of clubs. Then he leads the ten of diamonds to dummy's ace.

South pitches a spade on the king of diamonds. This is the position when dummy plays the queen of diamonds:

NORTH
♠ J73
♡ Q
◇ Q62
♣ —

EAST
♠ Q8
♡ 7
◇ —
♣ 10954

What's going on? Has declarer forgotten to pull the last trump? I'm just about to ruff the queen of diamonds when it occurs to me to count declarer's hand.

South started with two clubs, one diamond and five hearts. That gives him a five card spade suit! No doubt, he bid the hearts first, intending to "reverse" later with the spades. Some players bid that way.

To set Six Hearts, the defense will have to win two spade tricks. It won't hurt for me to pitch a club on the queen of diamonds, for South will still be left with three spades. But if I were to ruff the queen of diamonds, I could jeopardize the defense if, for example, declarer were to overruff and play the ace and another spade. Upon winning the queen of spades, I would be endplayed, forced to give declarer a sluff and a ruff on a club return. Not me. I pitch a club on dummy's queen of diamonds.

This was the position when the queen of diamonds was led from dummy:

```
                        NORTH
                        ♠ J73
                        ♡ Q
                        ◇ Q62
                        ♣ —
        WEST                            EAST
        ♠ K102                          ♠ Q8
        ♡ —                             ♡ 7
        ◇ J98                           ◇ —
        ♣ J                             ♣ 10954
                        SOUTH
                        ♠ A965
                        ♡ K109
                        ◇ —
                        ♣ —
```

If East ruffs the queen of diamonds, declarer can overruff and play the ace and another spade. East wins the doubleton queen of spades and the forced club return allows declarer to ruff in hand, pitching a spade from dummy. Declarer then ruffs a spade in dummy and the South hand is high.

The complete hand:

NORTH
- ♠ J73
- ♡ AQ6
- ◇ AKQ62
- ♣ 86

WEST
- ♠ K102
- ♡ 54
- ◇ J9873
- ♣ J73

EAST
- ♠ Q8
- ♡ 732
- ◇ 54
- ♣ Q109542

SOUTH
- ♠ A9654
- ♡ KJ1098
- ◇ 10
- ♣ AK

The hand had a happy ending for the declarer. After winning the queen of diamonds, declarer ruffed a diamond back to his hand and led a spade to dummy's jack. West rose with the king of spades in order to "force the declarer" with a diamond. South later guessed to play for the drop of the queen of spades, rather than to smother the ten, and so he made the slam.

Partner was furious and I had to apologize to him for failing to ruff the queen of diamonds.

"You're right," I conceded after some discussion, "If I had ruffed the diamond we'd have set the hand."

Hand 41

THE TIRED MAN

YESTERDAY, I PLAYED BRIDGE ALL NIGHT. And this morning, I got up at 6:00 a.m. Here it is almost midnight and I am playing rubber bridge again. I hold:

♠ K86   ♡ AK   ◇ J954   ♣ QJ108

Neither side is vulnerable and I am first to bid. I open the bidding with One Club. West passes and partner responds One Spade. East passes and I rebid One No Trump. Partner raises to Three No Trump, which all pass.

NORTH	EAST	SOUTH	WEST
—	—	1♣	Pass
1♠	Pass	1NT	Pass
3NT	Pass	Pass	Pass

West leads the jack of hearts and North puts down this dummy:

NORTH
♠ AQJ9
♡ 65
◇ AQ7
♣ 9763

SOUTH
♠ K86
♡ AK
◇ J954
♣ QJ108

Too bad West led a heart. Now I won't have time to develop the clubs. To make Three No Trump, I must win three tricks in diamonds.

I win the jack of hearts in hand and lead a low diamond to dummy's queen, which holds. Could East be holding off with the king of diamonds? Hardly. For all he knows the queen of diamonds may be my ninth trick.

The normal way to continue the diamonds is to play the ace and then follow with a diamond toward my jack-nine. That line of play losses only when West holds four diamonds king-ten.

But I'm wondering if there could be any merit in re-entering my hand and running the jack of diamonds through West. I'm tired, but I should be able to determine which is better play.

Let's see. Either play will win three tricks when diamonds are divided three-three, when West holds the doubleton king, and when East holds the doubleton ten. But leading the jack of diamonds will gain an extra trick when West holds K-10-x-x and East holds 8-x, for then if West covers the jack of diamonds, I can lead toward the nine, making three tricks unless West started with K-10-8-x.

Having decided how to play the diamonds, I return to hand with the king of spades. When I lead the jack of diamonds, West covers with the king. Dummy's ace wins and East drops the eight. Now the seven of diamonds forces out my ten and my nine of diamonds is high.

The complete hand:

NORTH
♠ AQJ9
♡ 65
◇ AQ7
♣ 9763

WEST
♠ 43
♡ J1093
◇ K1062
♣ K42

EAST
♠ 10752
♡ Q8742
◇ 83
♣ A5

SOUTH
♠ K86
♡ AK
◇ J954
♣ QJ108

It's not at all obvious, but suppose the diamonds had been:

NORTH
◇ AQ6

SOUTH
◇ J954

If a diamond were led to the queen and East were to drop the seven, then declarer still should run the jack of diamonds through West on the second round, for playing the jack of diamonds would produce three tricks when East held the 8-7 doubleton.

□   □   □

"You're not leaving are you?" says the owner of the bridge club, "We need you."

"All right I'll stay. Midnight's too early to leave anyway," I reply.

Hand 42

A VISIT WITH
AN OLD FRIEND

DURING THE YEARS 1964 TO 1966, I lived in New York City and played a fair amount of duplicate bridge. My regular partner was a friend named Tom.

This story comes from a National Bridge Tournament on the East Coast more than ten years later. Halfway through the afternoon session, I notice my old friend Tom playing in another section. As soon as the round is over, I must say hello. It would be nice to visit after so many years. And perhaps Tom can join me for dinner.

Sitting East, I hold:

♠ 104   ♡ KQ3   ◇ A82   ♣ K10976

South, on my left, opens the bidding with One Club. Partner passes and North responds One Diamond. I pass and South rebids Two No-Trump. North raises to Three No-Trump and all pass.

The bidding has been:

NORTH	EAST	SOUTH	WEST
—	—	1♣	Pass
1◇	Pass	2NT	Pass
3NT	Pass	Pass	Pass

Partner opens with the jack of hearts. North puts down this dummy:

NORTH
♠ 963
♡ 74
♢ KQJ94
♣ Q43

EAST
♠ 104
♡ KQ3
♢ A82
♣ K10976

I cover partner's jack of hearts with the queen ands declarer ducks. The hearts are most likely 5-3-3-2 around the table, with South holding three hearts A-x-x.

The missing high cards are the Ace-King-Queen of spades, the Ace of hearts, and the Ace of clubs, all of which ought to be held by South to justify his Two No-Trump rebid. In addition, South may also hold the Jack of spades and/or the jack of clubs.

Most likely, therefore, South holds something like:

1. ♠ AKQx ♡ Axx ♢ xx ♣ AJxx

2. ♠ AKQ ♡ Axx ♢ xxx ♣ AJxx

It looks normal enough to return a heart at trick two, but a heart is the wrong play. If I were to return a heart, declarer would duck and win the third heart. Declarer could then cash the Ace, King, and Queen of spades and lead a diamond. Upon winning the ace of diamonds I'd be endplayed, forced to return either a diamond or a club away from my king to dummy's queen.

No, the hearts can wait. The correct play at trick two is a low diamond, to strip declarer of his diamonds before returning a heart.

The complete hand:

NORTH
- ♠ 963
- ♥ 74
- ♦ KQJ94
- ♣ Q43

WEST
- ♠ 8752
- ♥ J10986
- ♦ 1073
- ♣ 8

EAST
- ♠ 104
- ♥ KQ3
- ♦ A82
- ♣ K10976

SOUTH
- ♠ AKQJ
- ♥ A52
- ♦ 65
- ♣ AJ52

Partner plays a low diamond to show three. Declarer wins the nine of diamonds in dummy and continues with the king of diamonds to my ace. At this point, I shift back to hearts, playing the king and another heart to South's ace.

Declarer has no way to get dummy's diamonds, so Three No-Trump is set one trick. Had I continued the hearts earlier, declarer could have made Four No-Trump by ducking the hearts, cashing his spades and leading a diamond.

□   □   □

After the hand was over, I noticed that my friend Tom had completed play at his table. I then went over to say hello.

"What are you doing?" cries the director.

"Nothing," I reply, "I just came over to visit a friend I haven't seen for many years."

"We don't allow players to leave their tables without a good excuse. If you want to visit your friend, wait until the session is over," says the director.

Hand 43

A FOOLISH DOUBLE

THIS HAND COME FROM A RUBBER BRIDGE GAME in which I am playing with an aggressive partner against average opponents. With both sides vulnerable, I hold the following hand as South:

♠ AKQJ106   ♡ 97542   ◇ —   ♣ 63

Left hand opponent and partner both pass. East, on my right, opens the bidding with One Club. I overcall One Spade and West comes in with Two Clubs. North and East pass and it is my bid. In view of partner's silence, a game seems unlikely, so I bid only Two Spades. This appears to be a better bid than Two Hearts, for with spades as trump we will score 150 honors.

West competes again with Three Clubs and partner comes to life with Three Spades. East passes again and I must decide whether or not to bid game.

Partner's Trump Support

Partner's failure to raise to Two Spades earlier was undoubtedly based on a lack of proper trump support. North probably has only a doubleton spade. He could easily hold any of the following hands:

1. ♠ xx   ♡ QJx   ◇ AJxxx   ♣ xxx
2. ♠ xx   ♡ Axx   ◇ KQxxx   ♣ xxx
3. ♠ xx   ♡ Kxx   ◇ AJxxx   ♣ xxx

150

Any one of these hands would suffice for a competitive raise to Three Spades. And yet, Four Spades would have no play whatsoever with an original club lead by the defense. At first sight then, it looks as though I should pass Three Spades.

Partner's Club Distribution

Something keeps nagging me, however. On the auction, it's quite likely that East-West hold nine clubs between them. If so, partner will have a doubleton club. North's distribution could well be either 2-4-5-2 or 2-3-6-2.

Partner's Diamond Strength

But if North were 2-3-6-2, with enough values to compete to Three Spades, then he surely would have bid Two Diamonds earlier, over Two Clubs. In fact, North might well have bid Two Diamonds earlier if he had five good diamonds. Since partner didn't bid Two Diamonds earlier, I'm inclined to assume that he doesn't hold a six card diamond suit, nor five good diamonds. In fact I'm going to assume that partner's distribution is 2-4-5-2, with most of his strength in hearts. And since as little as

♠ xx   ♡ AJxx   ◇ xxxxx   ♣ xx

would offer an excellent play for game, I'm going to bid Four Spades.

West, angered by what he considers arrogant bidding, Doubles. He knows that his side holds the majority of the high cards. What he doesn't appreciate, however, is the fact that the hand belongs to us anyway.

All pass, so the bidding has been:

NORTH	EAST	SOUTH	WEST
—	—	—	Pass
Pass	1♣	1♠	2♣
Pass	Pass	2♠	3♣
3♠	Pass	4♠	Double
Pass	Pass	Pass	

West leads the four of clubs and North puts down the dummy I had hoped for:

NORTH
♠ 72
♡ AQ63
♢ Q7543
♣ 87

SOUTH
♠ AKQJ106
♡ 97542
♢ —
♣ 63

East wins the first two tricks with the ace and queen of clubs and returns a spade. The deuce of clubs did not appear, so I cannot place the clubs exactly, but I am sure that they are divided five-four.

I pull three rounds of trump, West showing with three spades and East with two. It looks normal now to lead a heart to the ace as a safety play against East holding a singleton king. I have plenty of entries to set up the hearts and Four Spades, Doubled, is cold as long as I hold the hearts to one loser.

But can East have a singleton heart? Let's see. East started with two spades and either four or five clubs. Now, if he had a singleton heart, then his distribution would be either 2-1-6-4 or 2-1-5-5. With either of these hand patterns, he surely would have opened the bidding with One Diamond rather than One Club. Therefore, East must have at least two hearts.

I lead a heart to the queen, which holds. The hearts break 2-2, so I make a vulnerable overtrick, doubled, which is worth an additional 200 points.

This was the complete hand:

```
                    NORTH
                    ♠ 72
                    ♡ AQ63
                    ◇ Q7543
                    ♣ 87
    WEST                            EAST
    ♠ 985                           ♠ 43
    ♡ KJ                            ♡ 108
    ◇ K962                          ◇ AJ108
    ♣ K1054                         ♣ AQJ92
                    SOUTH
                    ♠ AKQJ106
                    ♡ 97542
                    ◇ —
                    ♣ 63
```

There's a good lesson to be learned from this hand. When the opponents bid a voluntary game with less than normal amount of high cards, they probably have some distributional values to justify their bidding. Unless you have some clue that the cards do not lie well for your opponents, you should not double. It's foolish to double a hand merely because your side holds the majority of high cards.

Hand 44

A MINOR DISASTER

WHEN PLAYING RUBBER BRIDGE minimizing your losses is just as important as winning points.

Playing in a rubber bridge game with a partner of average ability, I hold as North:

♠ 2   ♡ Q97653   ◊ J108542   ♣ —

Though not much in the way of high cards, the hand has some promise.

Our side is vulnerable and my partner, sitting South, opens One Club. West overcalls One Spade. My hand is hardly worth a bid of Two Hearts, so I pass. East raises to Three Spades and partner comes in with Four Clubs. West Doubles and it is my bid.

Thus far, the bidding has been:

NORTH	EAST	SOUTH	WEST
—	—	1♣	1♠
Pass	3♠	4♣	Double
?			

Should I bid Four Diamonds, Four Hearts, or Pass? A takeout Redouble with a non-expert partner is, of course, too dangerous. Whatever I do, I'm sure that we're going for a big number.

Before making any call, I'm going to give some consideration to the probable distribution of the suits.

The Distribution of the Clubs

Partner ought to have seven clubs for his Four Club bid. West surely holds four clubs to Double, so I imagine that the clubs are divided 7-4-2-0 around the table.

The Distribution of the Spades

It seems likely that the spades are divided 5-4-3-1 around the table rather than 5-5-2-1 or 6-4-2-1. I don't think that West would be doubling Four Clubs if he held six spades. Nor does it seem likely from the auction that East holds five spades.

South's Distribution

I've been able to place partner with seven clubs and three spades. Most likely, partner's distribution is 3-2-1-7 or 3-1-2-7.

How Will Four Clubs Play?

Before considering a rescue bid, I should estimate what the likely fate of Four Clubs Doubled would be. Partner probably holds something like:

1. ♠ xxx ♡ x ♢ Ax ♣ AKJ10xxx

2. ♠ xxx ♡ Kx ♢ x ♣ AKQ10xxx

3. ♠ xxx ♡ Ax ♢ x ♣ AKJxxxx

I imagine that Four Clubs will go down three or four, doubled, for minus 800 or 1100.

How Will Four Diamonds or Four Hearts Play?

If I bid Four Diamonds or Four Hearts and catch partner with a singleton trump the hand could turn into an even greater disaster. Even if I catch partner with a doubleton honor, Four Diamonds or Four Hearts will probably go down at least three tricks, Doubled. And with West holding five spades and four clubs, East is undoubtedly stacked in the red suits. A rescue bid is therefore too dangerous, so I am going to pass.

The complete hand:

```
                    NORTH
                    ♠ 2
                    ♡ Q97653
                    ◇ J108542
                    ♣ —
        WEST                        EAST
        ♠ A10986                    ♠ QJ43
        ♡ A2                        ♡ K1084
        ◇ A7                        ◇ KQ6
        ♣ J976                      ♣ 42
                    SOUTH
                    ♠ K75
                    ♡ J
                    ◇ 93
                    ♣ AKQ10853
```

West led the ace of spades, so Four Clubs Doubled went down only three, with 100 honors for minus 700. This was an extremely good result when one considers what the likely fate of Four Diamonds Doubled or Four Hearts Doubled would have been.

The point to be stressed by this hand is that an attempt should be made during the auction to count partner's hand and the opponents' hands. Frequently, there are logical inferences to be drawn from the bidding which, when analyzed, will help considerably in making a close decision.

On this hand it would be possible to construct numerous hands in which South might only hold six clubs or only two spades. And therefore, South might well hold three diamonds or three hearts. But I still believe that South is likely to hold seven clubs and three spades on the given auction, in which case it's clearly right for North to pass Four Clubs Doubled.

Hand 45

AN EARLY DUCK

WHEN ONE ARRIVES at what appears to be a hopeless contract, then the only thing to do is to conceive of a lie of the cards which will allow the contract to be made and then play for that lie of the cards to exist.

Playing in a rubber bridge game against good players, I am fortunate enough to hold:

♠ 5　♡ AKQJ1083　◇ A54　♣ Q7

With both sides vulnerable, partner opens the bidding with One Club! This looks like my lucky day. I jump to Two Hearts and partner responds Two Spades. Over Four No-Trump, partner responds Five Hearts, two aces. If partner has two kings, I'm going to bid a grand slam! But no, over Five Diamonds partner responds a disappointing Six Diamonds, one king only. I must settle for a small slam, so I bid Six Hearts.

The bidding has been:

NORTH	EAST	SOUTH	WEST
1♣	Pass	2♡	Pass
2♠	Pass	4NT	Pass
5♡	Pass	5NT	Pass
6◇	Pass	6♡	Pass
Pass	Pass		

West leads the queen of spades and this dummy appears:

NORTH

♠ AK73
♡ 4
♢ 8763
♣ A853

SOUTH

♠ 5
♡ AKQJ1083
♢ A54
♣ Q7

Partner's hand is indeed a disappointment, far worse than any I could have conceived he might hold. Not even a ten spot on the outside! And partner's king would have to be the king of spades.

We have eleven tricks on top and almost no chance of winning twelve tricks. I suppose I could win the ace and king of spades and race off all my trumps. Then I could play the ace and another diamond, hoping to endplay the opponent holding the king of clubs. But either of my opponents is quite good enough to foresee the endplay and unblock in diamonds. No, that won't work.

How about winning the king of spades in the dummy and ducking a diamond? Then I might be able to bring off some sort of a squeeze. The trouble is that my opponents could win the diamond in either hand and then a club shift or even a diamond a diamond continuation might ruin all chances of a squeeze.

This hand is driving me crazy. There must be some legitimate play for Six Hearts. How about a squeeze against West? That's a possibility. If West holds five spades and the king of clubs, then I can squeeze him.

But first, I'll have to lose an early trick. I have it! I'll duck the queen of spades! That will rectify the count and it will also prevent East from gaining the lead and breaking the squeeze with a club shift.

After winning the first trick West considers his next play for some time. Eventually he continues with a second spade. I win in dummy, pitching a diamond from hand. When I run off all of my trumps, West is squeezed as I had hoped, for the complete hand is :

NORTH
♠ AK73
♡ 4
♢ 8763
♣ A853

WEST
♠ QJ1084
♡ 96
♢ Q102
♣ KJ4

EAST
♠ 962
♡ 752
♢ KJ9
♣ 10962

SOUTH
♠ 5
♡ AKQJ1083
♢ A54
♣ Q7

The most difficult part of the hand was to conceive of the squeeze against West as the best chance to make Six Hearts. To execute the squeeze, declarer must duck a trick to rectify the count. It was best to duck the first trick, for if East obtains the lead he can break up the squeeze by returning a club.

If West had held six spades rather than five, he could set the hand by playing the king of clubs at the second trick. Declarer would be forced to play dummy's high spades before pulling trumps, and East would ruff the third round.

160

Once West plays a second spade, South need only guess who holds the king of clubs, for if East holds the king of clubs, the end position will be:

NORTH
♠ K7
♡ —
♦ 8
♣ A8

WEST
♠ 108
♡ —
♦ Q10
♣ J

EAST
♠ 9
♡ —
♦ KJ
♣ K10

SOUTH
♠ —
♡ 3
♦ A5
♣ Q7

When South leads his last trump, West discards a club, North discards a club, and East pitches a spade. Now a club to dummy's ace squeezes West out of a diamond and the king of spades squeezes East.

Hand 46

PLUS 200

"LET'S PLAY OUR JUMP OVERCALLS like a weak two bid," said my partner prior to the first round of an Open Pairs event. I agreed.

On the third round, playing against good opponents, I pick up the following hand in the North position:

♠ 97   ♡ J1092   ◇ AK1083   ♣ 43

Both sides are vulnerable. West, on my right, opens One Diamond and I pass. East responds One Heart and partner comes in with One Spade. West raises to Two Hearts. This is passed around to my partner who bids Two Spades. West passes and I pass, but East competes with Three Hearts which South and West pass to me.

The bidding has been:

NORTH	EAST	SOUTH	WEST
—	—	—	1◇
Pass	1♡	1♠	2♡
Pass	Pass	2♠	Pass
Pass	3♡	Pass	Pass
?			

At duplicate bridge a score of plus 200 can be a top board in a part score battle. The question is, should I Double, seeking plus 200 for a good match point score, or should I bid Three Spades, or pass?

Partner and I play our weak two bids, and hence our jump overcalls, as good as:

1. ♠ AKJxxx ♡ xx ◇ xx ♣ xxx

2. ♠ KQJxxx ♡ xx ◇ Kxx ♣ xx

3. ♠ AQJxxx ♡ x ◇ xxx ♣ Kxx

Partner's bidding in this auction must be based on a better hand than any of these, otherwise partner would have bid Two Spades immediately over One Heart. That makes a Double very attractive on first sight, for I hold three defensive tricks myself and partner certainly ought to take two tricks on the defense.

Before doubling, however, I pause to consider the likely distribution of the various hands.

South's Distribution

Partner should have a six card spade suit. Unless the opponents are mad, they surely have eight hearts between them, so partner will have a singleton heart. Partner's most likely distribution, therefore, is 6-1-3-3, or possibly, 6-1-2-4.

West's Distribution

On the auction, West ought to have a balanced hand. Since he opened One Diamond, rather than One Club, West surely holds four diamonds. Most likely West's distribution is 2-4-4-3, 2-3-4-4, or possibly 3-3-4-3.

The Distribution of the Diamomds

It's reasonable to assume that the diamonds are distributed 5-4-3-1 around the table rather than 5-4-2-2. Since West holds four diamonds and I hold five diamonds, East will have a singleton diamond whenever South's distribution is 6-1-3-3.

East's Distribution

If East has a singleton diamond, and it's likely that he has a singleton to compete to the three level, then his distribution ought to be 3-5-1-4, 3-4-1-5, or possibly 2-5-1-5.

How Will Three Hearts Play?

Too well, perhaps. If East holds a singleton diamond, as I suspect, then I will be limited to two tricks on defense and I'd have to rely upon partner to take three tricks to set Three Hearts.

How Will Three Spades Play?

Very well indeed. Especially if partner's distribution is 6-1-3-3, for then I shall probably have three tricks for him in diamonds.

After all this though, I finally decide on a bid of Three Spades. This is a good choice, but it turns out to be an underbid, for the complete hand is:

```
                NORTH
                ♠ 97
                ♡ J1092
                ◇ AK1083
                ♣ 43
WEST                              EAST
♠ J10                            ♠ 432
♡ A54                            ♡ KQ876
◇ Q976                          ◇ 2
♣ AQ92                          ♣ J1065
                SOUTH
                ♠ AKQ865
                ♡ 3
                ◇ J54
                ♣ K87
```

Playing in Three Spades we were plus 200 the hard way. West led the ace of hearts, after which the defense could not prevent declarer from winning eleven tricks. Three Hearts was doubled at several tables but it was never set.

Hand 47

AN UNETHICAL
OPPONENT

THE UNETHICAL PLAYER is most effective with his Doubles. He Doubles in three distinct tones. The first is a soft quiet double, which is for take out and asks partner to bid his best suit. The second tone is a hesitant Double, slightly louder than the first, designed to convey to the doubler's partner that the partner is puzzled as to the best course of action. This type of double asks the doubler's partner to take charge, either by passing for penalties or by bidding his best suit. The third type of Double is a loud determined tone which commands the doubler's partner to pass.

Playing rubber bridge with one of these distinctive tone doubler's at my right, I deal myself the following:

♠ 32   ♡ 7   ◊ KQJ108653   ♣ 62

Both sides are vulnerable. Since I have no defense, I open the bidding with Four Diamonds. West passes and partner raises me to Five Diamonds. East Doubles in a soft tone, for take out. This is passed around to my partner who Redoubles! I hope partner knows what he is doing. Both opponents give this some consideration, but neither ventures a bid, so Five Diamonds Redoubled becomes the final contract.

The bidding, hardly typical in our game, has been:

NORTH	EAST	SOUTH	WEST
—	—	4 ◇	Pass
5 ◇	Double	Pass	Pass
Redouble	Pass	Pass	Pass

West, looking rather unhappy, leads the deuce of hearts. Partner, full of pride, puts down this dummy:

NORTH
♠ A965
♡ KJ10
◇ A94
♣ AQ10

SOUTH
♠ 32
♡ 7
◇ KQJ108653
♣ 62

Not bad at all! With a sure heart trick, five diamonds is cold no matter how the cards lie.

I play dummy's ten of hearts and East wins the queen. He tries to cash the ace of hearts, but I ruff. I pull two rounds of trump, ending in dummy. Meanwhile, East shows void, pitching two hearts.

How shall I play for an overtrick? Right hand opponent surely holds the king of clubs. The best chance for an overtrick is to pitch a club on the king of hearts. Now I run my trumps, hoping to catch East on some kind of pseudo squeeze. Who knows perhaps he'll come down a doubleton king of clubs which I can ruff out.

After playing three rounds of trumps a rare squeeze comes to mind. I hadn't considered it, but if West holds the jack of clubs and East holds the king, then I can make an overtrick on a double criss-cross riffle diffle trump squeeze.

Sure enough, this is the position when I lead my penultimate trump:

```
                    NORTH
                    ♠ A9
                    ♡ —
                    ◊ —
                    ♣ AQ10
    WEST                              EAST
    ♠ Q8                             ♠ KJ
    ♡ —                              ♡ —
    ◊ —                              ◊ —
    ♣ J84                            ♣ K97
                    SOUTH
                    ♠ 32
                    ♡ —
                    ◊ 53
                    ♣ 6
```

West, forced to keep three clubs to prevent me from running the queen of clubs through East, pitches a spade. Dummy also pitches a spade and East is squeezed. Justice! That'll teach East to double me in a soft tone.

The complete hand:

NORTH
- ♠ A965
- ♡ KJ10
- ◊ A94
- ♣ AQ10

WEST
- ♠ Q84
- ♡ 8432
- ◊ 72
- ♣ J843

EAST
- ♠ KJ107
- ♡ AQ965
- ◊ —
- ♣ K975

SOUTH
- ♠ 32
- ♡ 7
- ◊ KQJ108653
- ♣ 62

This type of trump squeeze is extremely rare and easy to miss. Playing bridge regularly one might expect to encounter it in alternate decades.

Hand 48

A SLIP
IN THE PLAY

PLAYING RUBBER BRIDGE, I HOLD:

♠ AQJ10954　♡ A2　◊ 957　♣ 42

I open the bidding with Four Spades. West passes and partner, sitting North, raises me to Six Spades, which all pass.

The bidding has been:

NORTH	EAST	SOUTH	WEST
—	—	4♠	Pass
6♠	Pass	Pass	Pass

West leads the king of hearts and partner puts down this dummy:

NORTH
♠ 87
♡ 5
◊ AK1064
♣ AK973

SOUTH
♠ AQJ10954
♡ A2
◊ 97
♣ 42

170

The hand looks simple enough. I win the ace of hearts, ruff a heart in dummy, and continue with the ace and queen of spades. No matter how the spades divide, I have twelve top tricks.

West wins the second round of spades with the king and East discards a heart. West shifts to the queen of clubs which I win in dummy with the king, East dropping the jack.

I can't tell for sure how to exit from dummy at this point. But it looks more likely that West began with a singleton queen of clubs rather than a singleton diamond. Therefore, I play the ace and king of diamonds, planning to ruff a diamond to hand and pull West's last trump. Unhappily West ruffs the second round of diamonds, so I go down one in Six Spades.

The complete hand:

```
                    NORTH
                    ♠ 87
                    ♡ 5
                    ◇ AK1064
                    ♣ AK973
    WEST                            EAST
    ♠ K32                           ♠ 6
    ♡ KQ93                          ♡ J108764
    ◇ J                             ◇ QJ532
    ♣ Q10865                        ♣ J
                    SOUTH
                    ♠ AQJ10954
                    ♡ A2
                    ◇ 97
                    ♣ 42
```

I slipped in the play of this hand. After ruffing a heart in dummy, I should have cashed dummy's ace of clubs and ace of diamonds before playing the ace and the queen of spades. Had I done so West, upon winning the king of spades, would not have been able to make me guess how to exit from the dummy.

A NECESSARY OVERTRICK

PLAYING DUPLICATE BRIDGE with an inexperienced partner, I hold:

♠ AKJ942   ♡ K2   ◇ A83   ♣ 95

Partner opens the bidding with One No-Trump! I wish this were rubber bridge. It seems that all my slams are reserved for duplicate. I bid Three Spades, but partner rebids Three No-Trump. I'm bidding a slam anyway. I bid a direct Six Spades, which ought to be somewhat safer than Six No-Trump with partner at the helm.

The bidding, hardly scientific on my part, has been:

NORTH	EAST	SOUTH	WEST
1NT	Pass	3♠	Pass
3NT	Pass	6♠	Pass
Pass	Pass		

West hesitates for some time before selecting an opening lead. Eventually, he leads a trump. Partner contributes:

NORTH
♠ Q5
♡ A873
◇ K42
♣ AK62

SOUTH
♠ AKJ942
♡ K2
◇ A83
♣ 95

Wrong contract. We have twelve top tricks in Six Spades, for plus 980. And at the other tables the contract will probably be Six No-Trump, making six, for plus 990. To get a good match-point score on this hand, I'll have to make an overtrick. And that can be accomplished only by means of a squeeze.

Let me think about the hand for a moment. I can ruff a heart and a club and thus establish two threats against my opponents. Yes, that seems reasonable, for then if the last heart and the last club are held separately, I can make all the tricks on a double squeeze.

I play three rounds of trump, pitching a diamond from dummy.

The trumps split three-two. I continue with two rounds of hearts and ruff a heart. West shows with the 9-6-5 of hearts and East with the J-10-4. When I cash two clubs and ruff a club, West shows with the Q-10-8 and east with the 7-4-3.

The missing heart is the queen. So far I can see, there is no clue in the opponents' play which would indicate it's location. On the other hand East must hold the missing jack of clubs, for if West held the Q-J-10-8 of clubs, then he certainly would have led a club rather than fidget so long before selecting his opening lead.

The position now is:

```
                    NORTH
                    ♠ —
                    ♡ 8
                    ◇ K4
                    ♣ 6
    WEST                            EAST
    ♠ —                             ♠ —
    ♡ Q                             ♡ —
    ◇ Q107                          ◇ J96
    ♣ —                             ♣ J
                    SOUTH
                    ♠ 2
                    ♡ —
                    ◇ A83
                    ♣ —
```

The lead of the last trump squeezes both defenders. So I make an overtrick, for plus 1010, which yields a good match-point score.

The complete hand:

NORTH
♠ Q5
♡ A873
◇ K42
♣ AK62

WEST
♠ 73
♡ Q965
◇ Q1075
♣ Q108

EAST
♠ 1086
♡ J104
◇ J96
♣ J743

SOUTH
♠ AKJ942
♡ K2
◇ A83
♣ 95

It was essential to ruff both a club and a heart. By ruffing, declarer exhausts one opponent of the suit and establishes a threat against the other defender. A similar procedure can be used to good effect with A-x-x-x opposite a singleton. By ruffing twice, it's possible to establish a threat whenever the suit is divided 6-2 or 5-3.

A COLORFUL AUCTION

THIS IS ANOTHER HAND in which an analysis of the bidding indicates a course of action not readily apparent.

Playing in the Mixed Pairs of a Sectional Tournament, I hold the following hand as South:

♠ A97653   ♡ 732   ◇ —   ♣ KQ93

Neither side is vulnerable. East, my right hand opponent, opens One Diamond. I add some color to the auction with a pass. My left hand opponent is a girl in her early twenties. She responds One Heart and East rebids Two Clubs.

Now I come in with Two Spades. West bids a cheerful Three Diamonds, undoubtedly four card support. Partner passes and East bids Three Hearts. I come in again with Three Spades, but this produces no reaction from West. She bids an immediate Four Hearts, which is passed around the table to me.

Thus far the bidding has been:

NORTH	EAST	SOUTH	WEST
—	1◇	Pass	1♡
—	2♣	2♠	3◇
Pass	3♡	3♠	4♡
Pass	Pass	?	

East's Distribution

From the auction, East ought to be 1-3-5-4 or 1-3-4-5.

The Distribution of the Hearts

The hearts must be divided 4-3-3-3 or 5-3-3-2 around the table, for with a six card heart suit West probably would have bid Three Hearts over my Two Spade bid. Come to think of it, it's unlikely that West would risk playing a 4-3 fit, for she's clearly an inexperienced player. I assume, therefore, that West has five hearts.

West's Distribution

The diamonds are probably divided 5-4-4-0 around the table. Since I've been able to place West with five hearts and four diamonds, it's likely that her distribution is 2-5-4-2 or 3-5-4-1. West can't be very well fixed in spades, for if West had a good spade holding, she surely would have given some consideration to a Double of Three Spades. Instead, West bid an immediate Four Hearts over Three Spades. It's likely, therefore, that North holds the king or queen of spades.

North's Distribution

What about partner's distribution? The spades must be divided 6-3-3-1 or 6-4-2-1 around the table. Partner should hold three or four spades, including an honor, a doubleton heart, four or five diamonds, and either three or four clubs.

How Will Four Hearts Play?

Very well, I imagine. Even if partner manages to find the diamond lead and give me a ruff, we might be unable to set Four Hearts.

How Will Four Spades Play?

Will it play well? Yes, indeed! The most we should lose is one trump trick, two hearts, and a club. Of course we might go down three if West leads a singleton club and manages to negotiate two or three club ruffs. But that's a risk I'm willing to take. I bid Four Spades with some apprehension. West DOUBLES and partner frowns. If I have then taken a phantom save, I'll never hear the end of it. But partner's hand is most suitable.

NORTH
- ♠ K82
- ♡ 86
- ◇ 106542
- ♣ A65

SOUTH
- ♠ A97653
- ♡ 732
- ◇ —
- ♣ KQ93

West leads the king of hearts. This holds and she switches to a diamond, which I ruff. I duck a heart and ruff the diamond return.

When I lead the ace of spades, East drops the jack. I'm sure now that East's distribution is 1-3-4-5, so I lead a club to dummy's ace and finesse the nine of clubs on the return, making Four Spades, Doubled.

The complete hand:

NORTH
- ♠ K82
- ♡ 86
- ♢ 106542
- ♣ A65

WEST
- ♠ Q104
- ♡ KQJ95
- ♢ Q974
- ♣ 4

EAST
- ♠ J
- ♡ A104
- ♢ AKJ8
- ♣ J10873

SOUTH
- ♠ A97653
- ♡ 732
- ♢ —
- ♣ KQ93

"You sure were lucky," exclaims East, "to find your partner with three spades to the king, a doubleton heart, and the ace of clubs." I have to agree.

Hand 51

PRESSURE PLAY

PLAYING RUBBER BRIDGE, I hold as South:

$$\spadesuit \text{ A106} \quad \heartsuit \text{ KQ1065} \quad \diamondsuit \text{ KQ53} \quad \clubsuit \text{ 4}$$

I open the bidding with One Heart. West passes and North raises me to Two Hearts. East passes and I make a game try with Three Diamonds. West passes and partner jumps to Four Hearts which all pass.

The bidding has been:

NORTH	EAST	SOUTH	WEST
—	—	1♡	Pass
2♡	Pass	3◇	Pass
4♡	Pass	Pass	Pass

West leads a low heart and North puts down this dummy:

NORTH
♠ K93
♡ J987
◇ 82
♣ AJ93

SOUTH
♠ A106
♡ KQ1065
◇ KQ53
♣ 4

181

Dummy's seven of hearts wins the first trick, East playing low. The heart lead is bad news. On any other lead, I could ruff two diamonds in dummy. West probably has the diamonds behind me as well as the ace third of hearts and he has lead a heart to prevent me from ruffing diamonds in dummy.

Still, there's nothing to do at this point but lead a diamond to the king. West wins the ace and, as expected, he plays the ace and another heart. I win the third heart in hand. Meanwhile, East discards two spades.

East's two spade discards show that he began with five spades. Most likely, his distribution is 5-1-3-4, which gives West a distribution of 2-3-4-4.

I have nine top tricks consisting of two spades, four hearts in hand, a diamond, a diamond ruff in dummy, and the ace of clubs. If I am to win a tenth trick, it will have to be on some sort of a squeeze.

I need to concede a third trick to the opponents to get a squeeze position. I have threat cards in both spades and diamonds which I do not want to give up. Therefore, I lead a club to dummy's nine.

East wins the ten of clubs and returns a diamond. I win the queen of diamonds in hand and ruff a diamond in dummy. Both opponents follow to the third round of diamonds, which leaves West with the last diamond. I ruff a low club to hand, which leaves the following position:

```
                    NORTH
                 ♠ K93
                 ♡ —
                 ◇ —
                 ♣ AJ
    WEST                          EAST
 ♠ J5                          ♠ Q87
 ♡ —                           ♡ —
 ◇ J                           ◇ —
 ♣ Q8                          ♣ K7
                    SOUTH
                 ♠ A106
                 ♡ K
                 ◇ 5
                 ♣ —
```

I lead my last trump, which puts pressure upon West in three suits. He can't discard a diamond, or my last diamond will be high. Nor can he let go of a club, for then East would be squeezed in the black suits. West is therefore forced to discard a spade.

I lead a spade to dummy's king and cash the ace of clubs, pitching a diamond from hand. On the return, I finesse the ten of spades, making Four Hearts.

The complete hand:

NORTH
♠ K93
♡ J987
◇ 82
♣ AJ93

WEST
♠ J5
♡ A43
◇ AJ94
♣ Q865

EAST
♠ Q8742
♡ 2
◇ 1076
♣ K1072

SOUTH
♠ A106
♡ KQ1065
◇ KQ53
♣ 4

Hand 52

PLEASING
SQUEEZING

LIKE ALL BRIDGE PLAYERS, I enjoy executing a squeeze, especially when there are some complications to the play.

Playing in my regular rubber bridge game, I hold as South:

♠ A9872   ♡ KQ87   ◇ A82   ♣ 2

We are vulnerable and I am first to bid. I open the bidding with One Spade. West passes and North responds One No-Trump. East passes and I rebid Two Hearts. Partner raises me to Three Hearts and I bid game.

The bidding has been:

NORTH	EAST	SOUTH	WEST
—	—	1♠	Pass
1NT	Pass	2♡	Pass
3♡	Pass	4♡	Pass
Pass	Pass		

West leads the four of clubs. Partner puts down this dummy:

NORTH
♠ 54
♡ J1052
◇ K43
♣ A765

SOUTH
♠ A9872
♡ KQ87
◇ A82
♣ 2

I win the ace of clubs in dummy and lead a spade. East plays the king and I win the ace. On the second round of spades West shows out, pitching the three of clubs.

I have a good chance for ten tricks on a cross ruff if East fails to return a trump at this point. But no! East wins the ten of spades and plays a heart. West wins and returns a trump. This is the position when West returns a trump:

NORTH
♠ —
♡ J105
◇ K43
♣ 765

SOUTH
♠ 982
♡ KQ8
◇ A82
♣ —

If the spades had divided 4-2 or if East had failed to return a trump, Four Hearts would have been cold. As it is, however, I have only nine tricks. And with the spot cards I've been dealt, my only chance to make Four Hearts is on a squeeze. But before I can squeeze my opponents, I'll have to concede a third trick.

West appears to have five clubs. Most likely, his distribution is 1-3-4-5 or 1-4-3-5. I'll have to assume that he is 1-3-4-5, for if he holds four hearts I'll be down no matter how I continue.

I already have a spade threat against East. Now if I were to ruff two clubs, I could set up a threat against West. Yes, I think I can do it if I win the jack of hearts in dummy.

East follows the second heart, which is good, for the hearts could have divided 4-1. I ruff a club to hand and lead a spade. West pitches a diamond and I must discard a diamond from dummy on the spade, for this is my only chance to lose a trick and yet maintain the threat in spades.

East wins the spade. Fortunately, he doesn't have the missing trump. After winning the spade he thinks for some time and finally decides to return a diamond. I win the diamond with dummy's king and ruff a club to hand. The position now is:

```
                     NORTH
                     ♠ —
                     ♡ 105
                     ◇ 4
                     ♣ 7
     WEST                                EAST
     ♠ —                                 ♠ QJ
     ♡ 9                                 ♡ —
     ◇ J9                                ◇ Q10
     ♣ K                                 ♣ —
                     SOUTH
                     ♠ 98
                     ♡ —
                     ◇ A8
                     ♣ —
```

I lead a spade toward dummy. West chooses to retain his trump and discards another diamond. I ruff the spade and cash dummy's high trump, squeezing East in diamonds and spades.

The complete hand:

```
                     NORTH
                     ♠ 54
                     ♡ J1052
                     ◇ K43
                     ♣ A765
     WEST                                EAST
     ♠ 3                                 ♠ KQJ106
     ♡ A93                               ♡ 64
     ◇ J965                              ◇ Q107
     ♣ K10843                            ♣ QJ9
                     SOUTH
                     ♠ A9872
                     ♡ KQ87
                     ◇ A82
                     ♣ 2
```

It was essential to win the second trump in dummy in order to ruff two clubs. By ruffing clubs twice declarer exhausts East of the suit and sets up a threat against West. Thereafter, declarer ducks a spade to East and makes Four Hearts on a double squeeze.

Hand 53

THE BRIDGE CLONE

MY RIGHT HAND OPPONENT IS AN AVID BRIDGE PLAYER.
She attends every local tournament. She's also a Bridge
Clone, incapable of original thought but well trained in
regurgitating tournament bridge dogma.

Sitting West I hold:

♠ 65 ♡ KJ2 ♢ 6542 ♣ 10653

South, at my right, opens the bidding with One
Diamond. I pass and North responds One Spade. With
partner and I silent throughout the bidding, the opponents
reach Three No-Trump on this auction:

NORTH	EAST	SOUTH	WEST
—	—	1♢	Pass
1♠	Pass	2♠	Pass
3♡	Pass	3NT	Pass
Pass	Pass		

It's my lead. Clubs are the unbid suit and a club lead
looks normal. But before making any lead, I'm going to
give some thought of the likely distribution of the suits and
the likely play of the hand.

North's Distribution

North's bidding of One Spade followed by Three Hearts suggests that North is 5-4 in the majors. Since North passed Three No Trump, rather than correct to Four Spades, North's most likely distribution is 5-4-2-2. Further, it's likely that North holds an honor in clubs, otherwise, she still might have bid Four Spades over Three No-Trump.

The Distribution of the Spades

On the auction, North ought to have five spades. South surely holds three spades. The spades, therefore, must be 5-3-3-2 around the table.

South's Distribution

Since South opened the bidding with One Diamond, rather than One Club, she surely holds four or five diamonds. South could have bid One No-Trump over One Spade. Instead, South chose to raise to Two Spades with only three spades. It's likely, therefore, that South holds a small doubleton in hearts and one or two honors in spades. South's distribution ought to be 3-2-5-3, 3-2-4-4, or possibly 3-1-5-4.

The Distribution of the Diamonds

The diamonds ought to be divided 5-4-2-2 around the table. On this auction, I make it slightly more likely that declarer holds five diamonds rather than four.

How Will Three No-trump Play?

Three No-Trump ought to play very well for our opponents. Any missing diamond honors that are held by partner will be well placed for declarer. In view of my poor spot cards in diamonds, it's likely that declarer will be able to run the suit.

Further, with the spades dividing 3-2, it's likely that declarer will also be able to win four or five tricks in spades. In short, while partner and I may hold eight clubs between us, a club lead will be too slow in establishing tricks for the defense. On the bidding, our opponents surely hold two clubs stoppers between them and declarer is likely to run both the diamonds and the spades before we cash any clubs.

Should I Lead a Heart?

The hearts are probably divided 4-4-3-2, or possibly 5-4-3-1, around the table, with partner holding at least four hearts.

Further, South's rebid of Two Spades, in preference to One No-Trump, was probably made due to a weak heart holding. With a doubleton heart honor, South might well have rebid One No-Trump rather than Two Spades.

If I lead a heart and catch partner with either the ace or the queen, then the defense will be able to set up and cash some heart tricks before our opponents run both the spades and the diamonds. A heart lead is surely better than a club.

Which Heart Should I Lead?

The lead of a low heart may cause the heart suit to block if partner holds the queen-nine or the ace-ten. At rubber bridge, I would have to give some consideration to leading the jack of hearts, for the hearts might well be:

                        NORTH
                        ♡ Q843
WEST   **EAST**
♡ KJ2   ♡ A1076
                        SOUTH
                        ♡ 95

Here the lead of the jack of hearts permits the defense to win four tricks in hearts, while the lead of the king of hearts would yield only three tricks. At rubber bridge, the jack of hearts might be the better lead.

At duplicate bridge, however, I think the king of hearts is the better lead. I don't need to shoot for the maximum result. All that I need is for a heart lead to produce one extra trick for the defense, which will yield us a good match point score. And the lead of the king of hearts has one advantage over the jack; the king of hearts might pin a singleton queen.

The complete hand:

NORTH
♠ AJ943
♡ A984
◇ Q8
♣ K7

WEST
♠ 65
♡ KJ2
◇ 6542
♣ 10653

EAST
♠ K87
♡ 107653
◇ K9
♣ Q82

SOUTH
♠ Q102
♡ Q
◇ AJ1073
♣ AJ94

The king of hearts proves to be the killing opening lead. After this lead, the defense wins a spade and two hearts. On any other lead, declarer would win twelve tricks.

□　　　□　　　□

After the session ends a friend of mine informs me that the Bridge Clone was telling everyone I cheated her by leading the king of hearts and that I must have seen the hand being played at another table to have made this lead.

For the moment, I felt quite angry. After all, no one likes to be accused of cheating. Being an attorney, I reflect upon my legal training. Since I am also a professional bridge player and earn part of my income playing bridge, the Bridge Clone's accusations of cheating constitute Slander. I could sue her if I wanted.

194

But I don't feel like pursuing the matter. It's not worth the trouble. And in any event, when one plays tournament bridge and wins, one must expect to be accused of cheating. Unfortunately, accusations of cheating are part of the game.

Hand 54

A MISSING SUIT

THERE ARE A LOT OF INFERENCES that can be drawn from an auction in which a suit is never mentioned. Occasionally, it becomes possible to count all the hands at the table.

Playing in a rubber bridge game with three players who are known to be weak, I deal myself the following hand as East:

♠ 4   ♡ AQ82   ◇ 6532   ♣ K1083

Both sides are vulnerable. I pass, South and West pass, and North, at my right, opens One Club. I pass and South responds One Diamond. Partner comes in with One Heart and North bids One No-Trump. With the king of hearts well placed, Three Hearts seems to be the right bid now, for it puts a lot of pressure on my left hand opponent. And Three Hearts may be effective in shutting out the spade suit.

South, however, refuses to concede and bids Four Clubs. Partner passes, North bids Four Diamonds, and it is my bid.

Thus far, the bidding has been:

NORTH	EAST	SOUTH	WEST
—	Pass	Pass	Pass
1♣	Pass	1◇	1♡
1NT	3♡	4♣	Pass
4◇	?		

The Distribution of the Spades

Let me think about the hand for a moment. I wonder what happened to the spade suit. North can't have a five card spade suit, for then he surely would have bid them some time. South can't have a five card spade suit either, for if South had five spades, he would have responded One Spade over his partner's One Club bid. Finally, in view of partner's One Heart overcall on what appears to be a jack high suit, I'm sure that partner doesn't have a five card spade suit either. In fact, the spades must be divided 4-4-4-1 around the table.

North's Distribution

What about North's distribution? I know that he holds four spades. Surely, his shape must be either 4-2-3-4 or 4-3-3-3. North can't have a four card diamond suit, for if North had four diamonds he surely would have opened the bidding with One Diamond rather than One Club. And North can't have a four club suit either, for then North would have passed Four Clubs rather than take a preference to Four Diamonds with only three. Hence, North must be 4-3-3-3.

South's Distribution

South holds four spades. It's unlikely that partner has a six card heart suit, so South will have a singleton heart. South's other cards must be either five diamonds and three clubs or four diamonds and four clubs. Would South have bid Four Clubs with only three clubs support? Certainly not. If South's distribution were 4-1-5-3, he would have bid Three Spades over my Three heart bid rather than Four Clubs.

Hence, I'm going to place South with a distribution of 4-1-4-4.

How Will Four Diamonds Play?

I've discovered the opponents are on a 4-3 fit! And the hand with four diamonds is the hand that will be forced with hearts. Against Four Diamonds, I should be able to win the ace of hearts, a club trick and a trump trick by forcing declarer to ruff a heart. That's book in my own hand. And since partner has overcalled with a jack high suit, it's likely that he has some outside strength, probably in spades. And with the spades breaking 4-1 for the opponents, I'd be surprised if partner didn't take at least two tricks on defense. Clearly, I have a sound Double of Four Diamonds.

All pass Four Diamonds Doubled, so the bidding has been:

NORTH	EAST	SOUTH	WEST
—	Pass	Pass	Pass
1♣	Pass	1♦	1♥
1NT	3♥	4♣	Pass
4♦	Double	Pass	Pass
Pass			

Partner leads the ten of hearts. The dummy is just about what I had expected:

NORTH
♠ A865
♡ KJ3
♦ J98
♣ AJ2

EAST
♠ 4
♡ AQ82
♦ 6532
♣ K1083

198

Dummy covers the ten of hearts with the jack and I win the queen. I shift to a trump, declarer ducks and partner wins the king. Partner returns a second heart, which declarer ruffs. Eventually, Four Diamonds goes down three, Doubled.

The complete hand:

```
                    NORTH
                    ♠ A865
                    ♡ KJ3
                    ◇ J98
                    ♣ AJ2
     WEST                              EAST
     ♠ KQ93                            ♠ 4
     ♡ 109654                          ♡ AQ82
     ◇ K7                              ◇ 6532
     ♣ 74                             ♣ K1083
                    SOUTH
                    ♠ J1072
                    ♡ 7
                    ◇ AQ104
                    ♣ Q965
```

After the hand, I was able to compliment partner for his discretion in passing the Double, for his good defense, and of course for his brave lead directing overcall.

THE CAPRICIOUS COMPETITOR

SOME BRIDGE PLAYERS like to compete in every auction. Their objective seems to be to play as many hands as possible rather than to achieve the best possible results. On some hands their unwarranted bidding helps the declarer considerably in the play of the hand.

Playing rubber bridge, I hold the following hand as South:

♠ KJ42   ♡ A2   ◇ A103   ♣ A1052

We are vulnerable and they are not. After two passes, I open One No-Trump. West overcalls Two Clubs, natural. North bids Two No-Trump, East passes, and it is my bid.

Partner's bidding is usually sound. On this auction his bid of Two No trump ought to be based on at least seven or eight points. I don't have much extra for a 16 to 18 point One No-Trump opener, but I do have two club stoppers. And I hate to miss a vulnerable game, so I bid Three No-Trump which all pass.

The bidding has been:

NORTH	EAST	SOUTH	WEST
Pass	Pass	1NT	2♣
2NT	Pass	3NT	Pass
Pass	Pass		

West leads the five of spades. Commenting that perhaps he ought to have bid Two Hearts, rather than Two No-Trump, partner puts down:

NORTH

♠ A3
♡ KJ653
◇ 654
♣ 963

SOUTH

♠ KJ42
♡ A2
◇ A103
♣ A1052

Dummy is no better than I deserve. Still, these 24 point games do come home once in a while.

I play low from the dummy and win East's seven of spades with the jack. That gives me seven tricks on top. How am I going to win nine?

It seems that the best chance to develop two extra tricks lies in the heart suit. I can win four tricks in hearts when the suit breaks 3-3 or when West holds the doubleton queen.

From the bidding and the opening lead, it's likely that West holds four spades and five clubs. If so, then the hearts will break 3-3 only when the diamonds are 6-1 and West's distribution is 4-3-1-5. That seems unlikely. Is there a better line of play than to attack hearts?

West surely would have led a club if he held K-Q-J-x-x. His lead of a spade virtually marks East with a singleton honor in clubs. That means I can develop an eighth trick by cashing the ace of clubs and leading a club toward dummy's nine.

It's more likely that West's distribution is 4-2-2-5 than 4-3-1-5. If I go after the clubs, then I may be able to squeeze or endplay East after conceding two clubs and a diamond. And if necessary, I can always fall back on the heart finesse for my ninth trick.

At trick two, therefore, I cash the ace of clubs. All is well, for East drops the jack. West wins the second club with the queen and returns a spade to dummy's ace. I force out the king of clubs. East, meanwhile, has pitched a diamond and a heart.

West continues with the queen of spades to my king. This is the position when I lead a low diamond:

NORTH
♠ —
♡ KJ65
♢ 654
♣ —

WEST
♠ 10
♡ 84
♢ KJ
♣ 87

EAST
♠ —
♡ Q109
♢ Q987
♣ —

SOUTH
♠ 4
♡ A2
♢ A103
♣ 10

West wins the jack of diamonds. If West fails to cash the ten of spades at this point I'll cash the ace of diamonds and the ace of hearts and then exit with a diamond endplaying East.

West cashes the ten of spades. No matter. I discard a diamond from dummy and East also lets go of a diamond. West then exits with a club. Dummy pitches a heart and East is squeezed in the red suits.

The complete hand:

NORTH
♠ A3
♡ KJ653
♢ 654
♣ 963

WEST
♠ Q1065
♡ 84
♢ KJ
♣ KQ874

EAST
♠ 987
♡ Q1097
♢ Q9872
♣ J

SOUTH
♠ KJ42
♡ A2
♢ A103
♣ A1052

West could have set the hand by leading hearts early, but it was a difficult defense.

If West had not entered the auction declarer would never have found the winning line of play. Where was West going anyway? His partner was a passed hand and One No-Trump had been bid at his right.

Hand 56

THE SUSPICION BOX

THIS STORY COMES FROM THE OPEN PAIRS of a Regional Tournament which was held several years ago in Pasadena, California. The local tournament committee had created a new device called the Suspicion Box to help eliminate "the vast amount of cheating" that goes on at bridge tournaments.

As advertised in the Daily Bulletin, anyone noticing suspicious activity was invited to deposit a written description of the questionable conduct, identifying the parties involved, into a large wooden Suspicion Box prominently displayed on one of the tables in the center of the playing area. Later, a committee of reputable players would investigate each written claim of misconduct.

"You know," says East, pointing to the Suspicion Box, "I think it's a great idea. Now it's going to be a lot harder to get away with cheating."

Personally, I thought the Suspicion Box was an abomination. But who was I to argue with the Forces That Be. And there was no use discussing the matter with East. East was just another Bridge Clone, incapable of original thought, but well trained in detecting and reporting suspicious activity.

Sitting South, I hold:

♠ 4   ♡ AK875   ◇ AQ75   ♣ K53

I open the bidding with One Heart. West makes a jump overcall of Two Spades, weak, and North competes with Three Hearts. East bids Four Spades and I bid Five Hearts, which all pass. The bidding has been:

NORTH	EAST	SOUTH	WEST
—	—	1♡	2♠
3♡	4♠	5♡	Pass
Pass	Pass		

West leads the deuce of diamonds and North puts down this dummy:

NORTH
♠ A
♡ 1042
◇ 10643
♣ Q10842

SOUTH
♠ 4
♡ AK875
◇ AQ75
♣ K53

This opening lead is an obvious singleton. I play low in dummy and win East's eight of diamonds with the queen.

Both opponents follow to the ace and king of hearts, West dropping the nine and jack of hearts and East following with the three and the six of hearts. This leaves the queen of hearts outstanding.

If West had been dealt the Q-J-9 of hearts, he probably would have led a spade rather than a singleton diamond. I am going to assume, therefore, that West was originally dealt two hearts and one diamond. West's remaining cards ought to be six spades and four clubs.

I lead a spade to dummy's ace and continue by leading a club to my king and West's ace. If I'm correct about distribution, East is out of clubs and I should finesse dummy's eight of clubs on the return. West ponders his return for some time. Eventually he selects a spade, giving me a ruff and a sluff. If I ruff in dummy, then I'll be forced to exit with a diamond from dummy, setting up two diamonds tricks for East. No, I must ruff the spade in hand.

I lead a club toward dummy's Q-10-8-x and finesse the eight, East showing void. Now a heart from dummy knocks out East's queen of trumps while I still hold the ace of diamonds and another trump. Later, I finesse the ten of clubs, pitching my two losing diamonds on dummy's clubs, so I make Five Hearts.

The complete hand:

```
                    NORTH
                    ♠ A
                    ♡ 1042
                    ◇ 10643
                    ♣ Q10842
     WEST                              EAST
     ♠ KJ10653                         ♠ Q9872
     ♡ J9                              ♡ Q63
     ◇ 2                               ◇ KJ98
     ♣ AJ97                            ♣ 6
                    SOUTH
                    ♠ 4
                    ♡ AK875
                    ◇ AQ75
                    ♣ K53
```

West does much better to lead a spade on the go. Without the diamond lead, which was marked as a singleton, declarer would have no chance to guess the distribution correctly. And unless declarer plays West for four clubs, Five Hearts must be set.

□　　□　　□

"Did you see that," says East, referring to Jim and Judy, husband and wife, each of whom was playing with another partner.

"See what," I reply.

"Jim left his table during the middle of the round, to talk to Judy," says the Bridge Clone.

"So what," I reply.

"They might have been discussing the hands," says the Bridge Clone.

"They also may have been discussing where to have dinner," I respond, trying to counter her doubts.

"It doesn't matter," says the Bridge Clone. "It looks suspicious to me and I am going to report it." And so she did.

Hand 57

LOCATING THE KING

PLAYING IN THE MIXED PAIRS of a Regional Tournament, I hold as South:

♠ KQ1095   ♡ K102   ◇ Q4   ♣ AQ6

I open the bidding with One Spade. West overcalls two diamonds and North makes a limit raise of Three Spades.

East passes and I bid Four Spades, which all pass.

The bidding has been:

NORTH	EAST	SOUTH	WEST
—	—	1♠	2◇
3♠	Pass	4♠	Pass
Pass	Pass		

West leads the king of diamonds and North puts down this dummy:

NORTH
♠ AJ87
♡ A8
◇ 7653
♣ 942

SOUTH
♠ KQ1095
♡ K102
◇ Q4
♣ AQ6

208

West cashes the king and ace of diamonds, East dropping the jack, and continues with a third round of diamonds. On the third diamond, East pitches a heart and I ruff.

I play the king and ace of spades. West shows void on the second round, pitching a low club and saving both of his remaining diamonds. I continue with the ace and king of hearts and a heart ruff to dummy.

East's first pitch of a heart was surely from five, so West started with five diamonds, three hearts, one spade, and therefore four clubs.

West began with one of these two hands:

  1. ♠ x ♡ Jxx ◇ AK109x ♣ Kxxx

  2. ♠ x ♡ Jxx ◇ AK109x ♣ Jxxx

In spite of his good diamonds, West might not have overcalled Two Diamonds without the king of clubs. In any event, I'm inclined to place the king of clubs with West rather than with East.

I could lead dummy's last diamond now, pitching a club from hand. Upon winning the diamond, West would be endplayed, forced to lead a club into my ace-queen or a heart for a sluff ruff.

The problem with leading a diamond, however is that East could foil the endplay by ruffing. If I'm right about the location of the king of clubs, then I can make Four Spades by continuing with a high trump from dummy.

Sure enough, this is the position when North cashes the jack of spades:

```
                    NORTH
                    ♠ J
                    ♡ —
                    ◊ 7
                    ♣ 942
     WEST                          EAST
     ♠ —                           ♠ 6
     ♡ —                           ♡ Q
     ◊ 102                         ◊ —
     ♣ K107                        ♣ J85
                    SOUTH
                    ♠ Q10
                    ♡ —
                    ◊ —
                    ♣ AQ6
```

If West discards a diamond, then a diamond from dummy endplays West to lead a club into declarer's ace-queen.

On the other hand, if West retains both diamonds, then the ace and a low club will drive out the king. Declarer need only guess which defender holds the king of clubs to make Four Spades.

The complete hand:

NORTH
♠ AJ87
♡ A8
♢ 7653
♣ 942

WEST
♠ 4
♡ J63
♢ AK1092
♣ K1073

EAST
♠ 632
♡ Q9754
♢ J8
♣ J85

SOUTH
♠ KQ1095
♡ K102
♢ Q4
♣ AQ6

Hand 58

HOMEWORK

THIS IS A HAND WHERE AN EARLY COUNT is absolutely necessary to achieve success in defense of a hand.

Sitting East in an IMP team of four game, I hold as dealer:

♠ K73   ♡ 2   ◇ AJ1096   ♣ AK42

Neither side is vulnerable. I open One Diamond. Left hand opponent overcalls One Spade. Partner leaps to Four Hearts and North, after deliberating for a while, bids Four Spades, which I Double.

The bidding has been:

NORTH	EAST	SOUTH	WEST
—	1◇	1♠	4♡
4♠	Double	Pass	Pass
Pass			

Partner leads the deuce of diamonds and North puts down this dummy:

NORTH
♠ J986
♡ A43
◇ K875
♣ Q9

EAST
♠ K73
♡ 2
◇ AJ1096
♣ AK42

Dummy plays low on the opening lead and I insert the nine of diamonds, which holds. Before making the obvious shift to a heart, I stop to do my homework.

Partner is marked with three diamonds. For his jump to Four Hearts, partner should have a seven card suit. His other three cards ought to be one spade and two clubs.

That gives South a five card club suit! I can see what will happen if I return a heart. We'll set up a heart trick, but we'll never cash it. Declarer will win dummy's ace of hearts and finesse the spades. Then he will force out my ace and king of clubs. Eventually, dummy's hearts will be pitched on South's good clubs and South will ruff his heart loser in dummy.

That is why I must play the ace, king and another club for partner to ruff. Dummy overruffs, but South later must concede a heart, for down one.

The complete hand:

```
                    NORTH
                    ♠ J986
                    ♡ A43
                    ◇ K875
                    ♣ Q9
    WEST                              EAST
    ♠ 5                               ♠ K73
    ♡ KQ109876                        ♡ 2
    ◇ Q42                             ◇ AJ1096
    ♣ 75                              ♣ AK42
                    SOUTH
                    ♠ AQ1042
                    ♡ J5
                    ◇ 3
                    ♣ J10863
```

At the other table the bidding was identical, but the opening lead was the king of hearts. The defense had no chance to set Four Spades.

Hand 59

THE ATTORNEY

PLAYING SOUTH in my favorite rubber bridge game, I hold:

♠ AK   ♡ AK654   ◇ AK6   ♣ A98

Although not much in the way of high cards, the hand has promise. North and East pass and I open the bidding with Two Clubs, strong and artificial. Partner and I soon reach Six Hearts on this auction:

NORTH	EAST	SOUTH	WEST
Pass	Pass	2♣	Pass
2◇	Pass	2♡	Pass
4♡	Pass	6♡	Pass
Pass	Pass		

West opens the queen of spades and North puts down a good dummy for me:

NORTH
♠ 8762
♡ Q832
◇ Q4
♣ Q103

SOUTH
♠ AK
♡ AK654
◇ AK6
♣ A98

I win the spade in hand with the king and lead the ace of hearts. Of course, there would be no story to tell if the hearts broke, for then I would have twelve top tricks. Naturally, West shows void on the first heart, pitching a diamond.

How am I going to win twelve tricks now? I can win three top hearts, three diamonds, two spades and two spade ruffs, and the ace of clubs, for a total of eleven tricks. On the surface, it looks as though I must lose a heart and a club no matter how I continue.

I suppose I could play East for the singleton king of clubs. The trouble is that West's diamond discard on the first heart figures to be from five. Hence West's most likely distribution is 4-0-5-4 and there's virtually no chance of catching East with the singleton king of clubs.

How about the endplay? That's a thought. If I ruff only one spade and strip East of spades and diamonds, then I could put him on play with the fourth round of hearts, forcing a lead into dummy's queen-ten of clubs. Even assuming that East holds the king of clubs, however, that would give me only two spades and a spade ruff, three hearts, three diamonds, and two clubs, for a total of eleven tricks. I'd still be one trick short of making Six Hearts.

Wait a minute! If I save a spade in dummy as a threat against West, I think I can force West to blank down to a doubleton club. Then if West holds the jack of clubs and East the king, I could win three club tricks by leading dummy's queen, pinning the jack.

Yes, Six Hearts is makable provided that East's distribution is either 3-4-3-3 or 2-4-3-4, with West holding the jack of clubs and East the king. And while my chances are slim, they are not nearly as remote as playing East for the singleton king of clubs.

I begin cashing the queen, king, and ace of diamonds, being careful to ruff the third round of diamonds in dummy, for I can't afford to pitch either a club or a spade from dummy on the third diamond. Next comes a spade to the ace, the ace and queen of hearts, and a spade ruff to hand.

This is the position when I lead my last trump to East's jack:

NORTH
♠ 8
♡ —
♢ —
♣ Q103

WEST
♠ J
♡ —
♢ —
♣ J65

EAST
♠ —
♡ J
♢ —
♣ K72

SOUTH
♠ —
♡ 6
♢ —
♣ A98

West is forced to pitch a club in order to protect his jack of spades against dummy's eight. I let go the spade from dummy, putting East on play with nothing but clubs. The forced club return allows me to bring home the club suit without any losers, so I make Six Hearts.

The complete hand:

NORTH
- ♠ 8762
- ♡ Q832
- ◇ Q4
- ♣ Q103

WEST
- ♠ QJ109
- ♡ —
- ◇ J9872
- ♣ J654

EAST
- ♠ 543
- ♡ J1097
- ◇ 1053
- ♣ K72

SOUTH
- ♠ AK
- ♡ AK654
- ◇ AK6
- ◇ A98

"If I live to be eighty, which I won't," says East, "I'll never understand how you made Six Hearts on this hand."

"As long as you're not planning to live to eighty," I reply, "How about letting me draft a Will for you. After all, I am an attorney."

Hand 60

A NEW FRIEND

I REALLY ENJOY PLAYING IN BRIDGE TOURNAMENTS because of the opportunities that frequently arise to make new friends with people that I otherwise would never meet.

While playing in a Regional Tournament, an attractive young lady sits behind me to kibitz. She's gorgeous. I sure would like to get to know her.

Sitting West, I hold:

♠ 105　♡ 832　◇ A63　♣ AJ874

South, on my right, opens the bidding with One Heart. I pass and North responds One No-Trump. Partner passes and our opponents bid to Four Hearts on this auction:

NORTH	EAST	SOUTH	WEST
—	—	1♡	Pass
1NT	Pass	3♠	Pass
3NT	Pass	4♡	Pass
Pass	Pass		

Before selecting an opening lead, I give some thought to the likely distribution of the North-South hands and the major suits.

South's Distribution

South, for his bidding ought to have five spades and six hearts. His most likely distribution is 5-6-1-1.

North's Distribution

North, having failed to raise either hearts or spades, ought to be 2-2 in the majors. His most likely distribution is 2-2-5-4.

The Distribution of the Hearts

It's likely that the hearts will be breaking 6-3-2-2 around the table. Therefore, a forcing game seems futile.

The Distribution of the Spades

The spades ought to be 5-4-2-2 around the table, with partner holding four spades. A trump lead will limit declarer to one ruff in dummy. Therefore, I am going to lead a trump, to protect partner's spade holding.

I lead the three of hearts and North puts down this dummy:

```
                    NORTH
                    ♠ 64
                    ♡ 109
                    ◇ Q1075
                    ♣ KQ653
    WEST
    ♠ 105
    ♡ 832
    ◇ A63
    ♣ AJ874
```

Partner plays the queen of hearts on dummy's nine and South wins the ace. Declarer continues with the ace and king of spades and ruffs a spade in dummy as I pitch a low diamond. Partner plays high-low on the spades, showing four, and on the third round of spades he follows with the jack. Next declarer plays the king of clubs from dummy, East the ten, South the nine, and I win the ace.

I'm sure now that South began with an original distribution of 5-6-1-1, for if South had a diamond void he probably would have ruffed a diamond to hand, picked up the trumps, and conceded a spade to partner's queen and club to my ace, making Five Hearts.

The ace, queen, ten, and nine of hearts have been played. Only the king and jack of hearts remain higher than my eight. My eight of hearts has taken on new prominence and it may become the setting trick. Since the hand has become a virtually a double dummy problem at this point, I may as well show all hands:

```
                    NORTH
                    ♠ —
                    ♡ —
                    ◇ Q1075
                    ♣ Q653
    WEST                            EAST
    ♠ —                             ♠ Q
    ♡ 82                            ♡ 6
    ◇ A3                            ◇ KJ984
    ♣ J874                          ♣ 2
                    SOUTH
                    ♠ 98
                    ♡ KJ754
                    ◇ 3
                    ♣ —
```

I underlead my ace of diamonds to partner's king-jack. Partner then cashes the queen of spades and I pitch the ace of diamonds! Now a diamond from East promotes my eight of hearts, so Four Hearts goes down one.

The complete hand:

NORTH
♠ 64
♡ 109
♦ Q1075
♣ KQ653

WEST
♠ 105
♡ 832
♦ A63
♣ AJ874

EAST
♠ QJ73
♡ Q6
♦ KJ984
♣ 102

SOUTH
♠ AK982
♡ AKJ754
♦ 3
♣ 9

"That was so neat," says the young lady kibitzing me, "I can't believe you pitched the ace of diamonds."

"I'm glad you enjoyed the hand," I respond.

"Let me introduce myself," she says, "I'm Betty."

"I'm Jim," I reply. "How about having dinner with me?"

"I'd love to," she replies. It was the beginning of a pleasant relationship.

Hand 61

AN EASY COUNT

IN SOME COMPETITIVE AUCTIONS it's possible to form an accurate picture of all the hands.

Playing rubber bridge, I am fortunate enough to hold the following hand in the South position:

♠ — ♡ 843 ◇ AKQ9 ♣ AKQJ97

Both sides are vulnerable and we have a part score of 60. West opens One Spade. Partner passes and East responds Two Spades. I come in with Three Clubs. The auction proceeds:

NORTH	EAST	SOUTH	WEST
—	—	—	1♠
Pass	2♠	3♣	3♡
Pass	4♡	5♣	5♡
Pass	Pass	?	

West hesitates for some time over my Five Club bid before bidding Five Hearts. Partner and East pass and it is my bid. Before deciding whether to bid on or Double, I give some consideration to the likely distribution of the hands and the suits.

The Distribution of the Hearts

The hearts must be distributed 5-4-3-1 around the table. East wouldn't have bid Four Hearts without four card support. And West surely has five hearts to rebid them at the five level.

This information alone makes Six Clubs a standout bid. But for practice, let's count the rest of the hand together.

West's Distribution

West is certainly 5-5 or 6-5 in the majors. His most likely distribution is 5-5-2-1.

The Distribution of the Spades

It's likely that the spades are divided 5-5-3-0 around the table. If East had four spades, he might well have chosen to bid Four Spades, rather than Four Hearts at his second opportunity to bid.

North's Distribution

Partner ought to hold five spades and a singleton heart. His most likely distribution is 5-1-4-3 or 5-1-3-4.

East's Distribution

East is 3-4 in the majors. He ought to be 3-4-4-2.

In any event, I'm not going to defend Five Hearts for a small penalty when there's a good chance of making a vulnerable slam. I bid Six Clubs. West, infuriated at my arrogant bidding, bellows a loud Double, which all pass.

The complete bidding has been:

NORTH	EAST	SOUTH	WEST
—	—	—	1♠
Pass	2♠	3♣	3♡
Pass	4♡	5♣	5♡
Pass	Pass	6♣	Double
Pass	Pass	Pass	

West leads the king of hearts. Partner puts down this suitable dummy:

NORTH

♠ 65432
♡ 2
◇ 653
♣ 6542

SOUTH

♠ —
♡ 843
◇ AKQ9
♣ AKQJ97

The appearance of this dummy is accomplished by some laughter. "Nice spot cards you've got there," says West. We shall see who gets the last laugh.

West's king of hearts holds the trick. Next he tries the ace of spades, which I ruff. When I cash the ace of trumps, West follows with the three and East plays the ten.

If West's distribution is 5-5-2-1, then I can make Six Clubs by ruffing two hearts and a diamond in dummy. On the other hand, there's East's ten of clubs to account for. East isn't the type of player who would falsecard at random from the 10-8 doubleton. And West's rather lengthy hesitation over Five Clubs is another indication that he may hold two clubs rather than a singleton.

If I play a second trump now and West was in fact dealt a singleton club, then I can still make the hand if West started with a doubleton jack or ten of diamonds, for after playing the ace and king of diamonds, I can establish a finessing position against East.

I cash another trump. As I rather expected, West follows suit. The hand is easy now. West started with 5-5-1-2 and East's distribution is 3-4-5-1. After cashing the ace of diamonds, I enter the dummy by ruffing a heart. On the return I finesse the nine of diamonds, Making Six Clubs, Doubled.

The complete hand:

```
                    NORTH
                    ♠ 65432
                    ♡ 2
                    ◇ 653
                    ♣ 6542
        WEST                        EAST
        ♠ AQJ108                    ♠ K97
        ♡ AKJ109                    ♡ Q765
        ◇ 7                         ◇ J10842
        ♣ 83                        ♣ 10
                    SOUTH
                    ♠ —
                    ♡ 843
                    ◇ AKQ9
                    ♣ AKQJ97
```

The picture I formed of the hand during the auction was off a card or two here and there. But on the whole, it was rather close to the actual holdings.

While West is moaning about the "freak distribution", I am wondering whether or not I would have made the hand if he had played a second heart at trick two. No, I think not, for I would not have known that an immediate finesse of the nine of diamonds was necessary.

Incidentally, even with a spade lead, Six Hearts Doubled costs only 400 as a save against Six Clubs, for West had "a hundred honors, in two suits."

The Complete Guide to
PASSED HAND BIDDING

In this major work, Mike Lawrence, the renowned World Contract Bridge Champion and teacher, presents the first modern, and thorough guide to all the options and weapons available when your side opens the bidding in third or fourth seat. About every situation that can occur in passed hand bidding is explained and copious illustrative examples are supplied.

Some questions dealt with include - When should one open aggressively in third seat? What does a fourth seat preempt look like? What does a passed hand jump shift look like? How to cope with competition? By exploring PASSED HAND BIDDING you will develop the judgment and methods to succeed in this critical area.

As a player, Lawrence has won three world championships - the Bermuda Bowl in 1970, 1971, and 1987. Besides winning scores of National and Regional events, Lawrence is a leading master point holder with the American Contract Bridge League and is a World Bridge Federation Grand Master.

As an author, Lawrence has written over ten bridge books, has his own bidding newsletter, and is a columnist for the American Contract Bridge magazine. Two of his books, How to Read Your Opponents' Cards and The Complete Book on Overcalls were named "book of the year" by Alfred Sheinwold and are considered classics.

PASSED HAND BIDDING by Mike Lawrence is a 200 page, 5 1/2" by 8 1/2", softcover book which retails for $12.95. The book can be ordered from Lawrence & Leong Publishing, 10430 Greenview Drive, Oakland, California. For mail orders add $1.00 for shipping & handling. (California residents please add applicable sales tax.)

CONTENTS